Praise for An Ordered Experience

Weaving together the personal with the universal, Timur Shah combines self-exploration with the timeless wisdom of story and myth. The result is by turns playful and insightful and shines with original talent. Let us hope there is more to come!

– Jason Elliot, author of *An Unexpected Light*

At once personal yet universal, learned yet not showy, original yet traditional, this is an exceptionally rich collection of meditations – narrative, essayistic, and autobiographical – on some of the greatest myths known to man. Beautifully written, attractively thoughtful, and achingly honest, *An Ordered Experience* is a remarkable debut that will delight anyone with a passion for mythology.

– Fitzroy Morrissey,
author of *A Short History of Arab Thought*

Flitting from Alexandria to an Antarctic research station and a British university town, this lively retelling of myths establishes Timur Shah as a highly original writer.

– James Von Leyden, author of *Last Boat From Tangier*

Timur Shah writes with a lively, thoughtful and accomplished new voice, bringing fresh resonance and personal perspective to ancient tales from folklore and mythology.

– Fiona Valpy, author of *The Storyteller of Casablanca*

In this lovely first collection, Timur Shah keeps the embers of our oldest stories glowing and reminds us that the value we find in ourselves (and what we can do) gives us hope and strength in a world not designed to serve our needs, preferences, or ideals.

– Mark Salzman, author of *Iron & Silk*

A remarkable and highly imaginative book from a dynamic young thinker and storyteller. I very much hope he has others on the way.

– JonArno Lawson, author of *Footpath Flowers*

Whether the setting is Ogygia, Antarctica or Tottenham Court Road, Timur Shah sends down buckets into the deepest wells of humankind's myths, and draws fresh stories and sparkling morals. Could there, for example, be an apter legend for the age of social media and its angsts than that of Narcissus and Echo?

'By adding to stories,' Timur writes, 'we are using them the way they were meant to be used.' He is right, and he has all the assets to add yet more, for us and for audiences to come.

– Tim Mackintosh-Smith, author of *Travels with a Tangerine*

In a strikingly original blend of scholarship and imagination, *An Ordered Experience* summons up some of the worlds great mythic pantheons and their stories and gives them new and personal meanings in modern life, thereby transforming doubt and failure into a literary triumph.

– Robert Irwin, author of *The Arabian Nights: A Companion*

A mercurial and erudite medley of epic retellings, short stories and literary analysis that playfully and poignantly underlines the endless adaptability of some of the world's greatest myths.

– Nick Jubber, author of *The Fairy Tellers*

A tour de force full of invention, interest and fine writing, Timur Shah is a fascinating young writer of great promise and potential.

– Robert Twigger, author of *Angry White Pyjamas*

From a distinguished family of storytellers and writers, an exciting new voice has emerged.

This is a wonderfully rich and quirky collection of short stories. Timur Shah has dipped into ancient mythology and folk tales, reworked them and turned them on their head. I was struck by the original take on old stories, from a chance encounter between Odysseus and Achilles in Hades, to a scientist conducting research in Antarctica who loses an eyeball, to a nervous university student who receives invaluable advice from Dionysus, to eating salad with Zeus, this is a vibrant mix of the bizarre and the fabulous.

– Richard Hamilton, author of *The Last Storytellers*

A sincere, hopeful, and heartfelt blend of essay and fiction by a preternaturally sensitive young writer who finds his voice – his voices – by engaging with classic myths, calmly determined to find the antidotes to the isolation and meaninglessness of our age.

– Josh Shoemake,
author of *Tangier: A Literary Guide for Travellers*

Timur Shah's book is an extraordinary and fascinating mixture: there are startlingly honest confessional essays about his insecurities, ruminations on myths and legends and their significance for him and for humanity in general, and a series of short stories into which the myths and legends seep. What is apparent throughout these diverse styles is that Shah, despite his own doubts about the fact, is a real writer. This is a terrific debut.

– Nigel Hinton, author of *Ship of Ghosts*

A uniquely kaleidoscopic and ambitious vision ranging across millennia connecting profound ancient myths to our transformed technological present.

– Michael Moran, author of *Beyond the Coral Sea*

This is an intriguing, poised, and creative debut from someone who truly understands the power and value of myth.

– Bijan Omrani, author of *Caesar's Footprints*

An Ordered
Experience

The Scheherazade Foundation

An Ordered Experience

TIMUR SHAH

The Scheherazade Foundation CIC
85 Great Portland Street
London
W1W 7LT
United Kingdom

www.SF.Charity
info@SF.Charity

First published by The Scheherazade Foundation CIC, 2023

AN ORDERED EXPERIENCE

© TIMUR SHAH

TimurShah.com

Timur Shah asserts the right to be identified as the Author of the Work
in accordance with the Copyright, Designs and Patents Act 1988.
A CIP catalogue record for this title is available from the British Library.

ISBN 978-1-915311-34-4

For Ariane. Because why not?

Contents

Odysseus & Achilles: Legacy & Fate   1

Addendum   13

Ragnarök & Mortality   21

I, Eye   33

Arthur & Pantheons   59

My Brain on People   67

The Dark Blue Sky   103

Nut, Dalila & Fiction (& Me): A Tangent   119

On Echo   129

Luke   139

A Big Hero in a Bigger World   157

On Meaninglessness   169

Calypso & Time   177

Acknowledgements   193

Odysseus & Achilles:
Legacy & Fate

I walk not knowing where but do,

And think and don't – unleash, unrein

Long and familiar the view.

HADES WAS HELL.

At least, Odysseus thought so. Nevertheless, he sailed on. The seer knew the unknowable, and Odysseus yearned for a sliver of clarity.

Whispers surrounded him. Shades, all that remained of a life lived above, wandered the realm of the dead. Such was the fate of any mortal foolish enough to have enjoyed mediocrity in the realm of the living. Alas, they remembered none of this. Memory was a commodity afforded only to the superlatives.

Upon the banks of the Lethe, uncountable souls swarmed, clamouring for a drink. The icy liquid touched their lips, purging the memory of their lives. That was the deal. Rather than risk torture, the souls condemned themselves to perpetuate that mediocrity – to exist no more. Vanishing memories were torturous enough for the living, for it is only through remembering that we exist. That we *persist*.

Odysseus was all too aware of this. He stared at the souls from his stone ship, the infamous Pontikonisi, and tried in vain to banish the thoughts of death. Perhaps he could grasp immortality in that way.

As a soldier, Odysseus knew those thoughts had never done him much good. Death was a curse you spat at your enemy on the battlefield, anything more was a distraction. And yet he stood there, alone, mortality on his mind.

Am I to be like this in death, he thought, *a faceless shadow yearning for obscurity?*

It seemed doubtful to him, but the old king was apprehensive about what the Fates had in store for him. Odysseus was certain, though, that there were fewer legacies awaiting him in the Underworld worse than fading into irrelevance and insignificance – oblivion. He was a proud man, yes, but an accomplished one. Odysseus was the hero of his story and had shouldered the burdens that unfortunate title carried, but actions don't always reveal a character's mind. The song of the sirens still rang in his ears – sweet promises of glory and an immortal legacy.

He did not remember how long ago he had encountered those foul, intoxicating creatures of the sea. The adventures with his crew seemed several lifetimes, or pages, ago. But Odysseus knew the power of the river Lethe.

The desire to forget was an intense one that lurks within us all, and he suspected the river's spirit wasn't taking kindly to a living mortal on its waters. He adjusted tack and the cold wind of the Underworld complied, pulling him deeper into its grasp, closer to his goal.

Odysseus was not welcome here, and his survival was as unlikely as ever. But he needed answers, and those answers only Tiresias could provide. Heroes were bound to a knowledge of the moment and no more, but there were others with far-reaching eyes.

The seer, even in death, retained his power of prophecy, and for his good service to the god Apollo, had been afforded an afterlife in the Isle of the Blest.

* * *

Odysseus' ship soon met the shore. In the distance he saw the silvery palace of Hades, home of the lord of the dead. He thanked the gods that it wasn't an audience with The Unseen One he was after. The creatures and spirits that populated the god's domain had made no positive change to his divine temperament. It was always worse than ever.

Trudging up the banks of the river, Odysseus moved forward. It was a lesson he had been taught even as a child through stories; the only way to survive the Underworld was sustained momentum.

Each step was heavy, threatening to pull him down for good. Persistence was a well-worn trait of Odysseus' by this time, and so onward he marched. As he reached the isle, the journey grew easier. Tired, but reluctant to slow down so close to his goal, Odysseus kept up his determined pace. As he reached his destination, however, he spotted something that made him stop in his tracks.

It was as if he had seen a ghost, which, he surmised, he had. But Odysseus was certain. He could see a shred of humanity in the land devoid of it. Besides, those piercing grey eyes and the mop of black hair betrayed his identity immediately, even underneath the glimmering helmet.

Odysseus was normally a composed man, but catching sight of his long-dead ally caught him off guard. He looked away, scarcely able to believe it. Returning his gaze, Odysseus saw Achilles staring straight back at him, a curious expression on his face.

* * *

On a journey so riddled with surprises and twists of Fate, standing face to face as he now did with one of the greatest heroes of all just added to the list.

His features were as perfect in death as they had been in life. His armour, forged by the great Hephaestus, god of blacksmiths, radiated power, shimmering gold and bronze in the perpetually inky landscape.

Achilles took a step forward. It was only then that Odysseus noticed the army behind him: a sprawling mass of soldiers, a wild mix of ages and ethnicities. The army disappeared into the horizon, the dead that made up its ranks motionless, awaiting orders from their leader. It was he who spoke first.

'I did not expect to see you here so soon, Odysseus.'

His voice was exactly as the Ithacan remembered. Even, but powerful. You could still imagine it commanding legions of thousands, for it had done before.

'Lost for words? I suppose there's a first time for everything,' Achilles said, his lips curling into a faint smile.

Odysseus did not know what possessed him, but he lurched forward and hugged his old friend. Achilles looked slightly taken aback, and embraced Odysseus in turn.

A small table rose from the ground, a disc of black earth and dirt, with two simple stools next to it. Achilles let go of his friend and walked towards them.

'Come, *Your Majesty*. I suspect you have a lot on your mind.'

* * *

Odysseus knew he couldn't stay long; the Underworld was a treacherous place and he had a mission to complete, but he nonetheless took the seat opposite Achilles.

Sure in his decision, Odysseus still felt a small tug at the back of his mind, as if some primordial being were snaking its way into his memories, preparing to pull.

A few minutes longer wouldn't hurt, he thought. Whatever evil sought his soul would have to wait.

Achilles removed his helmet and placed it on the table as he sat down. Odysseus was once again struck by his beauty.

'The great Odysseus in the land of the dead. As grateful as I am to see you, your visit to this wretched place suggests the pursuit of something important. Knowing you, it's most likely knowledge you're looking for.'

Odysseus, overcome with pride in his friend, told Achilles of his quest.

'It's Tiresias you're after, then? Makes sense. He is Apollo's prized oracle, even now. Extremely powerful. Never been one for prophecies myself, though.'

Odysseus allowed himself a smile. 'I can't imagine why,' he said, 'prophecies carried but promises of glory for you.'

'Perhaps. But glory is not a universal desire. It is a symptom of divine intervention.'

While not a child of the gods, Odysseus knew all too well of what his friend spoke. Mortals were seen as little more than pawns in a game beyond their understanding. He paused awhile then uttered words that had reverberated as truth in his mind for several achingly pensive years.

'I imagine you hold a lot of resentment. Dying in a war you wanted no part in.'

Achilles thought for a second before saying, 'No. I am happy here. My mother tried to make me invulnerable. My father mistakenly interfered. Unspoken differences are never sustainable. I finally have balance.'

Odysseus recalled the story. Thetis fed her son, the baby Achilles, ambrosia – the food of the gods – before placing him in a blazing hearth to burn away his perishable human parts. The child's father, the mortal king Peleus, on finding out immediately snatched Achilles from the flames.

The magic had been interrupted, the spell broken, and the boy would always be on the precipice of immortality. Like Tantalus with his fruit, for Achilles such perfect power would remain perpetually out of reach – his tendon serving as a solid shackle of flesh and sinew, anchoring him to the will of the Underworld.

'You are the product of so much intervention,' Odysseus finally said. 'Even I am guilty of it.'

'I was looking for a fight. I had been trained for war. You finding me only hastened the inevitable.'

'But you are – were – more than just a warrior. You had skills beyond the battlefield – Chiron taught you music, philosophy.'

Odysseus could not help but think of his own son, Telemachus. It had always been his intention that the boy would never see war. He had him trained, yes, but to defend himself. Odysseus had been raised as a soldier from birth –

much like Achilles – and as nothing else. His intelligence outside the battlefield had been hard won and earned in spite of his father and his training, not because of it.

'You were just a child, filled with endless potential, and we took advantage of you. We poisoned your future. Agamemnon's war was not yours to fight. You were invaluable, yes, and perhaps more responsible for our success than any other soldier, but it was wrong.'

He was bursting with emotion, with guilt. Odysseus had been travelling, fighting for so long, and he struggled to see the fairness of it all. Memories seemed to serve little use here, blending together his exploits, all of them achingly devoid of a reason. He buried his face in his hands and felt the anger and shame rise in him as Achilles finally spoke.

'You think too much of yourself, old friend.' Odysseus looked up, desolation warping his rugged features. 'Fairness is a fickle thing, and believing in it is nothing more than delusion. Besides, if you hadn't brought me into the fight, someone else would have. Life is the slowest-acting poison of them all.'

Odysseus knew Achilles was right, but it didn't make him feel any better.

'We are mighty and powerless creatures, playing at the whims of gods. But that doesn't make our lives any less important, Odysseus. It doesn't change how we feel. You have a wife and a son that make you happy, and that happiness is real. So is the pain, but it must exist to give the good any meaning.'

Achilles looked to his left. A man in simple but beautifully adorned armour stood before the throng. He was smiling, a soft smile, but one Odysseus could never forget, even at the shores of the Lethe. Patroclus, at Achilles' side in life and death and now, forevermore.

Odysseus stood. 'You must be proud, brave Achilles. Even in the realm of spirits, you retain your regal and leading nature.'

'Perhaps. But, in truth, I would much rather be a paid servant in a poor man's house and be above ground than king of kings among the dead. Do not discount what you have, dear Odysseus, nor that you have so much still to come.'

Achilles joined his place at the head of the army, his expression solemn. He looked at his friend, his fellow hero.

'Heed the words of Tiresias – your journey is not yet over.' His eyes softened. 'And be safe, old friend. For my sake and for yours.'

Odysseus could not fathom how long he stood there, watching a remnant of his past cross over the murky horizon, yet he knew something was escaping his senses. He drew his thoughts together and once again felt the tug of the Underworld, threatening to pull him under.

Life was hell. But it was also everything else. And so, he marched on.

Addendum

Perfection is impossible to attain,

but dammit if I'm not deluded enough

to think I can.

His encounter with Odysseus in the Underworld is the last story in which Achilles appears after his death, having fulfilled his prophecies and cemented his legacy. Odysseus, however, was still far from reaching his home of Ithaca.

Tiresias would offer advice, at their meeting, on how to defeat monsters that awaited him, and how to survive the island of Thrinacia. His adventures in the *Odyssey* are as numerous as they are unforgiving to the homeward-bound hero, but they feel so independent to me, just as worthwhile as individual escapades.

The stories of Achilles and Odysseus are both long and extensive ones. I hesitate to even call them stories – they are much more than that. Like life, they are collections of tales and experiences, of lessons learned and battles lost. In this case, quite literally.

I started out wanting to focus on Achilles. Possibly the pinnacle of the legends, his life was a tragic one, and yet not the only tragedy in the larger epic of the Trojan War. I began by reading the fantastic 'accounts' of his life, and compiled a list of story beats I thought would be the most interesting to include.

What I was particularly drawn to was the relationship between divinity and mortality, and how the life of Achilles constantly toes the line between the two. The first part I thought relevant was something that preceded the hero, yet foretold his greatness. A prophecy from the great Titans Prometheus and Themis decreed that the son of the goddess Thetis would be immensely powerful, much more so than his father.

The significance I found in this was that the goddess was, at the time, being pursued by Zeus and Poseidon, powerful Olympians who rarely took no for an answer. In the wake of the prophecy, Thetis was free to choose 'the most pious man on the planet', the mortal king Peleus, to father her child. There's another version I enjoyed where it was not for any oracular reason that Thetis snubbed Zeus, but that it was simply out of respect for the sanctity of his marriage to Hera. I thought it lent a sense of empowerment, morality and agency to a story environment that often lacks it.

That was to be the start of my story – the prophecy of Achilles' greatness, the goddess forbidden to the gods, and the hero's birth to the mortal Peleus. It was my intention, at that time, to tell the story of Achilles in full, from beginning to end.

I had my little list that covered his entire life, and I thought myself capable of telling it. I tried several times to write that beginning but eventually stopped. I was not writing something long enough to do justice to the story in full, and I would have to find a way around it.

This was something I had desperately tried to avoid. I had in my mind a simple task to do, and was falling at the first hurdle. I knew any other form of story would take more effort and planning than I wanted to expend. I was right, in a small way, but more wrong than I could even imagine.

I had spent hours trying to craft that introduction, desperate to make it work, when my mind began to wander. I remembered a small part of Achilles' story – its end. More accurately, it was only part of the story of a different hero's life – the famed Odysseus. As he carried out his own journey, braving the Underworld seeking a prophecy, it is said that Odysseus met the hero Achilles. This was something I could not stop thinking about, but I wasn't sure why.

I considered awhile the parallels between the two heroes, the moments they shared together in each other's stories. The horrors they both endured. It was then that I realised I had a framing device, ripe with potential. As soon as I had that, the writing became easier.

Not only did I now have an unencumbered method and setting for my own story, but it was one that was a marked improvement from what I had originally tried to make work. Instead of condensing Achilles' life down into a few hasty plot points, I could frame it in the context of another hero, his contemporary, Odysseus. They knew each other, they fought together, and they provided me with an opportunity to dissect and discuss them both.

The immediate parallel I drew between the two was the relationship of each to the infamy they held in life and in death. Glory and legacy. Achilles had been a great hero, but out of expectation more than any desire for greatness.

That directly contrasted with Odysseus, who was extremely concerned with his legacy and how he would be remembered, as most mortals were and continue to be. Achilles, then, had not only that perspective going into their interaction, but the benefit of hindsight after death, and knowledge of what it was like to rest – a luxury not afforded to Odysseus for two decades.

In classic Greek fashion, there is a great deal of joy and tragedy in both their lives, and it was fascinating just thinking about the archetypes they upheld as characters in the same world. It was also, to a degree, intimidating writing about Achilles and Odysseus. Both have sustained remarkably in the public consciousness, and as a result of their longevity, feel almost like real people. Adding to their stories in my own way may have seemed that bit wrong, but I found it helpful to remind myself that that is what stories do.

Stories persist, they change and mutate, they teach and they make us feel. They are not above us, nor are we above them. They exist to provide a rickety bridge of understanding between cultures and times.

By remembering them we are blowing softly on embers that have glowed for most of recorded time, the extinguishing of which would serve as a late-stage oblivion. By adding to them we are using them the way they were meant to be used, and we are carrying on a tradition that has been alive for millennia – one that will outlive us all.

Ragnarök & Mortality

How will your gods fare in the inferno?

Will they succumb

to our mortal disease?

WHEN THE APPLES of Idunn are no more, when three winters pass with no summer, and the wolf Fenrir swallows the sun, Ragnarök will have come. It is the end of the world, the end of some of the most powerful gods.

The idea of a mythology with a built-in apocalypse is one I find fascinating. That interest can be boiled down, I suppose, to the consequential juxtaposition of figures of immense power with their certain weaknesses and demises. The notion of a god in prominent contemporary religion is typically associated with constancy and a lack of change. Especially as monotheism has become the prevailing belief within the world, it is understandable that the singular power of the god figure would be afforded an inherent superiority and permanence.

Many reasons have been suggested for the origin of myths, most of which appear to be no more than educated guesses. These range from the use of a myth as a teaching story, to the cultural veneration of individuals, to conveying wisdom and truths, culminating in the simple albeit reasonable idea that they served as collections of beliefs that were upheld as religious tenets.

I find it difficult, then, to conceive of a modern religion that would assert that the superhuman figures to which they ascribe their beliefs are capable of death or change at all.

Within Christianity, in the degree to which it can be

called a mythology, Jesus does die. I would argue, though, that my premise remains sound: his death is not permanent, and he is a manifestation of an already omnipresent God.

Another example I can think of to refute modern, mortal deities is Hinduism; there are gods therein that are capable of dying. A case, too, could be made for Hinduism incorporating the cycle of life and death within its deities, but I don't think this quite refutes my argument given that it is not a modern religion and in fact predates monotheism.

Firstly, the concept of what exactly a 'god' is in Hindu philosophy and teachings is much more nebulous than the admittedly rigid structure of most Western religions. More importantly, however, the 'death' of some of the larger deities such as Brahma or Vishnu could be more accurately characterised, I think, as adhering to a cycle of life, death and rebirth.

A broader point I would make, then, is that the greater the purported power and infallibility of a deity, the less populated is their pantheon, and the greater their immortal qualities tend to be within the stories from which they originate. Before I go on, though, let's go back to the beginning of the end.

In Norse mythology, Ragnarök is a series of events, including a great battle, that results in the destruction of the world and the death of many gods. The story of the apocalypse is told in the poem *Völuspá*, found in the 13th-century Icelandic manuscript known as the *Poetic Edda*. Ragnarök begins with the arrival of three giant children of the god Loki.

One of these giants, Fenrir, is an enormous wolf who will kill the god Odin during the battle. Another, Jörmungandr, is a colossal serpent whose task it is to poison the waters of the world. The third giant, Hel, is a goddess of the underworld whose role it will be to rule over the dead.

Unlike in Greek mythology, the Norse underworld serves less as a place in which souls are judged and treated accordingly. Unless one died in the midst of battle and went to Valhalla, they would 'live' a facsimile of a life in Helheim.

As the giants prepare for Ragnarök, though, the gods also make their preparations. The god Thor and his domain of thunder clouds will battle Jörmungandr, while the king of the gods, Odin, will face Fenrir. The god Freyr, typically associated with peace and a good harvest, will fight against the giant Surtr, who will emerge from the fire of the world to battle the gods.

Ragnarök will be a bloody and brutal battle, with much death and destruction. In the end, the gods will triumph, but at a great cost. Many of them will die, including Odin, Thor, Frey, and even the trickster god, Loki. The world will be destroyed, but it will be reborn again, and the cycle of life will begin anew, though perhaps less metaphorically than in Hinduism.

Ragnarök is not, then, totally fatal to the Norse gods. Those that die, though, are significant parts of Norse myths as a whole, and their ends are to be recognised as equally important. The belief in Ragnarök helped Norse people come to terms with their own mortality, and accept the inevitability of death.

No one was above death, not even the mighty gods. It also helped them to appreciate the beauty and fragility of life, and to live in the moment. In a culture where death was often seen as a natural and necessary part of life, Ragnarök served as a reminder that life was ultimately fragile and fleeting.

The same tone can be seen in another culture with its own version of a mortal god. The great Huitzilopochtli, war god and patron of the Aztecs, was the subject of great stories, and was a key figure in their system of beliefs. Although accounts of his origin differ, he is always portrayed as being instrumental in either the creation or sustained existence of humans.

It is said that fallen heroes and women who died in childbirth would serve this immensely powerful warrior, to be reincarnated as hummingbirds after four years. Already within the core of this myth there is a reference to death and impermanence, but the larger one comes at the end of his life. It was prophesied that with the death of Huitzilopochtli, so too would come the fall of the Aztec Empire. Not long after a temple of his in the capital burned down, the first Spanish attack descended upon Toxcatl, a sacred day of feasting dedicated to Huitzilopochtli.

This example goes to show a belief system that was more in line with and closely connected to its people. Not explicitly through the event – that can be easily chalked up to misfortune – but it demonstrates how the Aztec people were conscious of their own mortality and saw benefit in a religious system that reflected as much. Here, an immediate commonality can be seen between this and the Norse myths.

In the case of the latter, though perhaps not a reflection of the communities, the much more apparent parallel is a veneration of gods, and a belief in the stories of their power, coupled with the certainty that some of those gods would die.

I can find little reference as to what happens to the gods that survive Ragnarök. The realm of Helheim is unguarded, and the great warriors of Valhalla have served their final purpose. In the light of this unknown, there is a comic book series – Jason Aaron's 'Thor: The God Butcher' – that tackles this issue, and with explicit reference to the Norse myths.

I understand how juvenile the medium of comic books may seem, and I recognise the limits of that series to answer questions I have laid out in this essay. It remains, though, a captivating and entertaining exploration of the roles and fallibilities and powers of gods that I think is definitely worth a read.

It is this acknowledgement of power, though, and the fear that accompanies it, that I think is one of the more interesting things about Ragnarök. It is not simply the end of the world, but the end of the gods as well. This is a huge shift in power, and one that would have been accompanied by a great deal of fear and trepidation.

The Norse people were well aware of the might of their gods, and the potential for their powers to be used against them. In a world where the gods could die, anything was possible. Despite this fear, this self-created warning, there is still an aspect of Ragnarök upon which I have not yet touched – a more hopeful one.

Putting aside my discussion about the mortality of the gods, not all of them, as I wrote earlier, die during the events of Ragnarök. Freya and Sif, goddesses of love and the earth respectively, also survive, and are some of the highest-profile gods to do so.

An interesting survival, of sorts, is that of Baldr. The beautiful god of wisdom and light, though not strictly ascribed any domain, was killed long before the events of Ragnarök, in a plan orchestrated by the mischievous Loki.

Once the dust settles, he emerges from the Underworld, and he is once again in the realm of the living. This suggests to me a serious commitment to changing the nature of things and the circumstances of the gods. Not to mention the undoubtedly positive descriptions of Baldr (his name often translates as 'brave', 'strong' and 'shining') that add an air of hope to the world after Ragnarök.

Continuing on the subject of hope, there is more to be found after the Norse apocalypse. The three most feared monsters and giants – the wolf, the serpent and the goddess of the underworld, subjects of omens and portents – were gone. At the cost of the lives of great gods, evil just as great was defeated and dispelled from the Nine Worlds, which is the name given to the Norse universe.

Something, too, came in its place. Lif and Lifthrasir were the two humans told to have survived Ragnarök, though not much mention is given as to why they in particular remained. The story goes that they hid in Yggdrasil, the world tree, in the middle of Hoddmimir's Wood, and were sheltered there by the eagle that lived at the top.

This is significant for a number of reasons. The first is that it represents the survival of humanity after the destruction of the world, much like Noah in Christian mythology. The second is that it shows that even in the darkest of times, there is always some hope to be found.

The eagle is a symbol of hope and protection, and its presence in the story reaffirms the continuation and perseverance of nature. This is particularly meaningful given that it is told of Lif and Lifthrasir in the *Prose Edda*, that 'from them springs mankind'. There are casualties, there is loss, but there is, too, a well-founded hope. Humanity in the Norse myths were first descended from another pair, Ask and Embla, and the return of a pair in the events that follow Ragnarök suggests another great age to come.

Given the stories of the Norse, it seems safe to assert that the eternity of their gods was far more eventful. In comparison to a set of myths such as those of Ancient Greece, the Norse world seems to have fewer periods of stasis. The Greek stories have a sense of interminability, and while there are great changes that happen, they are cyclical in nature.

Ragnarök, on the other hand, is a cataclysmic event, one that signals the end of an age. It is the end of the world as the Norse people knew it, and the beginning of a new one. In this way, it seems that the Norse myths are more reflective of the human condition. We experience great change in our lives, and those changes can often be sudden and devastating.

The end of the world is a scary prospect, but it is also one that is full of potential. It is a time of great change, and with change comes opportunity. The stories of Ragnarök show us that even in the darkest of times, there is always some hope to be found. When the sun is swallowed by the wolf and the world is plunged into darkness, we can take comfort in the fact that the light will eventually return. And when the light does return, it will be all the brighter for having been extinguished.

I, Eye

Trust me when I say that being lonely

and being alone

are two very different things.

I LOVE MY routine. Not the individual components, per se, but as a whole, it's pretty great. My day always starts the same way. I wake up at around four a.m., because of the time difference – that's when mission control starts their day, too. But that doesn't bother me at all. It's not like there's much else to keep me occupied down here.

A small breakfast later – nothing fancy, just rehydrated porridge – and I'm at my desk working, usually by four-thirty. The commute isn't far, maybe ten feet. My bed, desk, 'kitchen' and 'toilet' occupy a space as big as a Winnebago. When I mention the latter two, I really mean a table with a kettle and some food, and a glorified bucket. I love it all. The space is my own.

Today marks seven months since I got here. Tomorrow, it will be seven months and one day. Those numbers describe my time here. I have done the same thing every day for seven months now, and I enjoy the whole that every facet of that routine creates. Every minute that made up those seven months is accounted for.

I sit down at my desk and download the equipment readings from last night.

'Okay, what've we got?'

Lines of data reveal themselves at their typically glacial pace – a dot matrix printer could have kept up. It doesn't bother me, though, it gives me enough time to peruse the lines as they come through. As they do, I turn on my desktop Christmas tree and watch the lights swell with their paltry energy. Maybe ten minutes later, I have the complete file in front of me. My connection's abysmally slow for some reason, but I eventually upload it to the central work hub and add my comment.

Data shows minor anomalous results. Equipment needs routine calibration.

This is one of the only 'out of routine' things for me, and it is more than enough to keep my need for novelty appeased. Once a month, I have to go outside and adjust some of the equipment. Nothing too complicated. The most annoying part of it is the half a dozen layers I have to put on beforehand, but that's a small price to pay to not freeze in Antarctic winds.

I factor this excursion into my plan for tomorrow. The equipment readings won't become an issue for another few days and besides, I already had a clear and simple idea of today – one I see no reason to mess with.

The connection on my computer isn't great. There's probably more than enough in the institute's budget to get a better network receiver, but it would take forever to get here and to set up, which seems like more effort than it's worth. All I use it for is data uploads and communication. I send the same emails to my colleague every day, confirming that I'm still alive and that everything's fine, and I get the same email back every day, too.

Hey Carol,
I'm here. The equipment's here. No angry leopard seals attacked me today. Fingers crossed about tomorrow.
-Sam.

The jokes are to amuse me more than anyone else. I'm the only audience I care about really, and down here that works fine. If the work wasn't so tedious, and I wasn't psychologically barred from doing so, I would stay in my little tundra-trapped bunk full-time. While I ponder my future, the response comes in. I don't need to read it to know what it says, but it's part of my routine, so I double-click on it.

Good work. Keep us posted.
-C

I sometimes wonder if they're more preoccupied with getting the data than making sure I'm alive. Like, I know, intrinsically, that's not true, but the thought interests me. I mean, they went to extreme lengths and efforts and costs to put up just this tiny outpost, and even if they picked me in a choice between saving me or the outpost, they'd hesitate.

For the next three hours, I do some really boring maths and graphic arrangements. Technically, I should have waited until this was done and sent it together with the data, but no one's complained so far, and I know they don't even look at the data until after lunch. They supposedly have other work to do.

None of the work is challenging. Anyone who paid attention in high school can do it, and if you've got a degree in data science and understand basic climate science, like I do, it's beyond simple. I do add the layer of panache that is submitting it as a PowerPoint file, if only to contribute a sliver of amusement knowing my bored colleagues on the other side of the world will be navigating a document with all of the senseless transitions I put in.

It's something that makes me smile, and down here, I've made instances of that happening as regular as possible. I am another cog in a machine that produces actionable truth, and it's my responsibility to myself to make that role as personally meaningful as I can. Currently, the jokes are the meaning. They seem like an iota of power I have over myself and potentially others, and that's a nice feeling.

But yeah, the work – mind-numbing. It's that cursed dichotomy of being so easy yet still requiring some focus, which means I can't even trust my autopilot to take over. Thankfully, I have my outing tomorrow, which I'm already looking forward to. On days on which I can't rely on that excitement, though, I turn to music and books. I like movies and shows fine, but downloading them with the poor connection is a bit of a bother.

It's just past eight-thirty when I finish my work. I add one more cheesy transition for good measure before uploading it to the hub. I check the status of the raw data file: unopened. I knew it.

Now comes possibly my favourite part of the day – second breakfast. I'll tell you, the hobbits were really on to something. I like it more than the other daily meals, just because it injects some whimsy into the time of day when my energy starts to sag. There's also some inner child that enjoys it so much, probably because I still associate breakfast with the sugary cereals of my youth. As I rehydrate some blueberries to put on my second bowl of porridge, I feel what's probably an unjustified amount of excitement.

This isn't exactly something born only out of reverence for the habits of Tolkien characters – I have to eat a lot of food to sustain my weight down here. The spread-out meals are my way of taking some ownership of that fact.

Also, it's a nice trip away from my desk, which sits at the wall opposite my 'kitchen'. I sit on my stool and finish my meal, taking far longer than I need to, though it's definitely time I have to spare.

I have a couple of hours before they'll get back to me, so I sit back at my desk and open my music app. I spent my first week here downloading three thousand songs, and they've been invaluable resources in keeping me entertained.

What I do in my first round of free time, which I have now approached, is compile a playlist. With as many songs as I have and as meticulously as I treat the project, organising a playlist of just fifty songs can take me up to an hour.

I use the music to curate or manage my emotions for the day. Some instrumental and classical tunes for when I'm working. Some upbeat songs for when I'm bored. Some sad songs if I'm a bit too happy and need to return to my baseline. It's a careful science, and I consider it just as important as the *actual* science I do here.

When I'm done, I label it with the date. I've saved every single playlist I've made since I got here, but never return to them. They serve as checkpoints of my time here, to be explored once I've left. In my outpost, though, the only one that matters is today's.

I'm listening to a track by Teddy Geiger when the first message from my parents comes in. Miming the twang of the guitar with my mouth, I open it. It's the usual.

Once a week or so, I'll hear from them. More often than not it's my mum, but my dad will check in whenever he has computer issues – he'd rather I troubleshoot it from the other side of the globe than look for outside help. It's never anything complicated, but it's always something new, so I oblige him. This time, though, it's just Mum.

Hey Sam,
Just wanted to check in. How's work going? How are you doing? We're so proud of you!

Love,
Mum (and Dad).

I respond with the usual.

I'm good. I'm doing good. The work is fine. I'm fine.
I miss you.

Love,
Sam.

It's not entirely a lie. I don't want them to worry, and I know this is what they want to hear. I am doing good, and the work is fine. I am fine. But, honestly, I don't really think about them outside of our brief messages.

The next message comes in an hour and a half later. I'm just making lunch and enjoying a high-tempo song by Watsky, and I spill boiling water on my hand. In my defence, the pouch of dehydrated beef stroganoff had an unreasonably small opening. It happens every couple of days, and it never hurts less.

I have my index and middle finger in my mouth like a teething baby when I hear the ping on my computer. Propping up the half-filled bag of stroganoff against the cursed kettle, I make my way to my desktop.

It was just a notification that Carol and the team had downloaded the file. That gives me about an hour before they get back to me, after no doubt enjoying my excellent presentation. They would send their assessment, assessing my work, and I would send an assessment of their assessment, to make sure we're on the same page. Riveting stuff. Anyway, I've got a lukewarm Russian lunch that isn't going to eat itself – unfortunately.

I switch sources of entertainment from music to audiobook. I finished listening to the works of Agatha Christie this week, and have just started the *oeuvre* of Conan Doyle. The tingling eeriness and dread that serves as a backdrop to so many of their stories is a great excitement when it's done right, but it's also more than capable of making a lunch less boring. I've got to find out who killed Enoch Drebber.

Soothed by the voice of Stephen Fry, I finish eating, wash up, and lie on my bed.

I used to spend this time exercising, but I've since learned to cling onto every gram of fat I put on. It wouldn't do me much good to be out in the cold without a natural layer of insulation, which I am sourcing courtesy of inactivity and gluttony. So here I am, in bed, blissfully aware of everything in my little habitat, wilfully ignorant of anything beyond it.

I am jolted out of relaxation by a loud *CRACK* followed by a long, agonising *CREEEAK*. It is muffled – outside. It isn't good, I know that, and what a fool I am for thinking anything would be. I have to go up there to have a look ASAP. Whatever's happened to the equipment is likely to get worse by the minute, and will only make my job more difficult tomorrow.

What's curious is that I didn't read any particularly high winds on my readings. That only makes me more eager to figure out what's actually going on. Whatever might have caused it is beyond my current understanding, and I don't want to risk this becoming more of a problem. Holmes will have to wait.

I consider letting Carol know but decide against it. Better I figure out what the problem is and come back with a solution. Now, though, it's time to suit up.

It's nothing as glamorous as the scenes in superhero movies in which the hero dons their costume for the first time, with swelling orchestral music. I get treated to the voice of Stephen Fry as I fumble to pause the audiobook, followed by several extremely unglamorous minutes of grunting and wheezing. Fifteen minutes, two parkas and several jumpers later, I'm ready.

There are two heavy metal doors that separate me from the elements. I make my way through half a foot of steel and then again, bracing myself before the final turn of the crank on the second. As the hinges relent, I am immediately greeted with fierce nature.

'Damn, it's cold,' I mutter into the wind.

As an inhabitant of Antarctica, that may seem inane. In truth, it is very easy for me to forget what it's like when it's cold. I'm rarely out here, and my current home was engineered with an absence of cold in mind. I grab a roll of cloth with loops containing the basics of a toolbox, and stuff it into a pocket at my side, before stepping out from my humble little airlock into the world.

The world is frozen, and white as far as I can see. I know there is water and a sea somewhere – it's how I got here – but now there is nothing. My gloves finding purchase on my goggles, I pull them down, covering my eyes. The light is less oppressive now. I have to head to the roof.

Facing the entrance to my habitat, the rungs leading up are to the immediate left. Access was always supposed to be easy. I plant my boot on the first rung and slowly begin to ascend. It's only eight feet or so to the top, but the gear I'm wearing to keep me from freezing does an excellent job at restricting movement, too – a trade-off I am of course more than happy to make. Nevertheless, it takes me a good ninety seconds before I'm sitting on the roof, my legs dangling over the edge as I wheeze and catch my breath.

Above, I am treated to more of the view, the blinding expanse. I wait for some semblance of strength to return before standing up and assessing the damage. My communications satellite dish has a small crack extending maybe an inch from the centre, where something must have hit it. It's nearly three feet in diameter, but I don't like the idea of leaving it out here to get worse.

Thankfully, the boffins that sent me here prepared for situations like this. At least, they sent another dish. It's in a box in the airlock, if I remember correctly. I take a deep breath before making my way back down, where I find it in the second box I pry open. The gloves didn't make anything easier by limiting my dexterity. I've barely got enough as it is.

I fasten the replacement dish to a carabiner at my waist and make the journey up to the roof again. It takes longer still, as I stop at every rung to prevent the dish from swinging and possibly getting damaged, too.

Panting, I heave myself back onto the roof, brushing some of the precariously formed ice from the surface. The three-legged stand that holds the faulty dish and most of the equipment I'm here to monitor is bolted firmly at each contact point, and isn't going anywhere. I grab it with my left hand and hoist myself into a standing position, putting the dish back into my field of vision.

Taking care not to damage it, I remove the spare dish from the carabiner and lay it by my feet. I then reach into my pocket, looking for a small wrench. Finding its handle, I pull it out and start loosening the arm holding the cracked dish. When I'm three-quarters done, I pull the arm towards myself gently, and am given a view of the cables running from its back through a box and down into my computer system.

All my data is being backed up constantly, so I know I'm not going to lose anything if I unplug the wires. So, I unplug the wires. This gives me the rest of the freedom of movement I need to remove the nut and final three screws holding up the cracked dish. I remove it and replace it in my hands with the undamaged one. Carefully, I align the dish on the stand and begin screwing it in. On the third screw, however, as I readjust my footing while tightening, my boot catches on a rogue piece of ice on the surface below me, and I pratfall.

Lying on my back, I'm almost tempted to laugh. My looped cloth turned makeshift utility belt had come undone and I was surrounded by various tools. Then, as I'm sitting up, I feel something sloshing in my goggles. The blood is warm and has completely submerged my left eye. I reach to remove the goggles and am met with instant pain, the kind I don't think I could withstand again, especially in this temperature. I start to stand up. I'm extremely dizzy.

The pain upgrades from unbearable, to excruciating, to a pulsing numbness. Still light-headed, I hold on to the stand in front of me for balance. My focus shifts, literally and figuratively. My right eye blinks a few times, a faint red slowly seeping into my peripheral vision. At the same time, it occurs to me what I am up here to do.

In a daze, I resume screwing in the dish. As I finish plugging the wires in, the pain returns, as does my attention. The brief stretch of autopilot has worn off and I'm back to bearing the weight of my nervous system.

The pain is worse than any I've felt before, and my head starts to feel heavy. I fight the mental fog for long enough to tighten the nut holding the stand, but my vision quickly blackens. I fall backwards, and the air is forced from my lungs.

* * *

The snow in Antarctica is not the same powder one knows as a child at Christmastime. It is an endless expanse, compact and dense – it is hard. Needless to say, not fun to land on. I suspect I've only been unconscious for a minute or two, which is still longer than I want to be while I'm out here. My body is pointed straight at the door to my precious hut – maybe three feet away.

Overcome by dizziness of all things, I force myself up and put a hand against the outside wall. I vomit and watch the colour of my bile mar the pristineness of the snow. Not feeling much better, I stumble inside. I grab the inner handle, and half-pull, half-fall in the direction of the sweet inside. Whatever it is, it does the trick. I repeat the same with the inner door and am greeted by warmth which, in my state, I interpret as extreme heat.

I take a few uneasy steps and stumble onto my bed, my head hanging over the side.

I'm once again reminded of the pain. The rest that I thought I'd be afforded at that point eludes me, and the throbbing is worse than ever. I have to fix whatever's hurting so much. Or try, at least.

I pull my gloves off with my teeth and remove the outermost and heaviest parka, throwing it off my body. I'm still unbearably warm but ignore it.

The pain is coming from my head. I can still feel liquid in my goggles, and I don't like what that means. Not knowing what else to do, I hold the goggles in place while removing the strap from the back of my head.

If there's a protocol for how to handle a situation like this, I don't know it, so I listen to the loudest voice in my brain that simply says: *Pull.*

In one sharp motion, I pull the goggles away from my face.

Aaaaaaahhhhh! Ow! Ow! Ow!

Let me translate: it hurts like hell. I'm suddenly wishing for the pain I felt outside, which feels like nothing compared to the searing agony that consumes me. Together with uncut panic, the two feelings rule my body until my subconscious makes the executive decision for me to pass out.

I remain unconscious for a while. I'm not sure how long this time, but it is long enough to take the pain down a notch from all-consuming to torturous, which is a step in the right direction. I no longer have the luxury of unconsciousness, and so do my best not to focus on the pain. It does not work. Still, though, I start to take stock of what's going on.

My gloves are in a small pile next to my desk and on the other side of the room; the parka I took off landed on my kitchen table, as in, the table that is my kitchen. It knocked over the thankfully empty kettle. That leaves the rest of my heavy outfit on me, from thermal underwear to jumpers to massive snow boots. That's when I look down.

Not at the trail of blood – that, I am expecting – but where it leads. In a small puddle of congealed, dark-red liquid sit my goggles. Punctured through one side is a screwdriver, which on the other side had impaled a small glob of pink and white mass. I slowly bend down to see what it is when I figure it out. What else could it be?

Lying in a pool of my blood is my left eyeball, with what looks like the optic nerve still attached. I am half-expecting it to start wriggling like a fish out of water, but it just sits there while I stare at it with my right eye.

It is more than safe to say that I am in a state of shock. Unable to process this information, it would seem, my brain decides to take the pain off my hands for a few minutes, which I use to slowly and dizzily find the first aid box. Not exactly sure what to do, I just grab a roll of gauze and start wrapping around my head and across my left socket. I go around and around a dozen times, until I start to feel the weight of it on my head. I fish for some pills in the box – I don't really care which – and absentmindedly swallow them.

All I feel now is a dull, strong ache, but at least it seems that I've managed the situation. I make my way over to my desk chair and take a seat. I let the blood rush in my skull for a while. Then, as a reminder that things can always get worse, I start hallucinating.

'Hello! I'm Mimir,' says the decapitated head floating in front of me.

'Nnnnnghh,' I groan. I have simply run out of bandwidth

to react appropriately.

'So, you've had your eye out? Classic. That's gotta hurt.'

I make eye contact with the head, hoping he registers my dwindling brain function. He seems not to notice and continues.

'How can I help, then?'

I don't move. I feel the gauze sticky against my skin. The head, undeterred, bobs in a circle, taking in the room. His scruffy grey hair and beard seem unaffected by gravity, but his expression changes as he makes his assessment. He turns to his right and takes in my screen.

'Ooh, what's this?'

Mimir scans his eyes over some text – my email inbox.

'Antarctica, eh? Looks like we're both pretty far from home.'

'Hooom?' I manage.

'Yeah, buddy.' He reads a bit more before turning to look at me. The childlike curiosity in his eyes is replaced with childlike concern. 'Oh gods,' he says. 'I completely forgot how people normally react to the whole eye part.'

Mimir looks at me sympathetically. 'Odin took it like a champ. He did it himself, though, which I imagine was helpful in managing the pain and surprise factor of it all. Also, he's a god, so it couldn't have hurt *that* much. You didn't do it yourself, did you?'

I furrow my brow.

'No of course not. Why would you have? It's not like you were expecting me.'

'Who... are... you?' The words take me an age to get out,

but at least my mental faculties are returning.

'Oh, I could have sworn I introduced myself. I'm Mimir – I'm kind of a big deal. Paragon of wisdom and all. And no, I'm not a hallucination. Yes, that is exactly what a hallucination would say, but I'm not having this whole argument again.'

I stare at him; there are no words queued in my brain to speak. So we sit there. Well, I sit. He hovers.

Mimir seems to notice my currently fractured consciousness, and so refrains from going on about himself. Even though I asked, I'm grateful for the silence.

'You don't need a biography right now, though, you need sleep.'

As soon as he says the word, my mind perks up. *Sleep – sounds like a good idea.* My eyelid(s?) doesn't start to get heavy or anything. One moment I'm awake – albeit barely functioning – the next, I'm in the deepest sleep of my life.

I wake up feeling unreasonably refreshed. I'm still in my chair, but the head isn't by my desk anymore. I touch my hand to the gauze; it's dry now, and I honestly feel no pain. That doesn't seem right. I turn in my chair a bit, and see the head over my bloody eyeball, inspecting it for who knows what.

'D-did you do something to my head? It feels, like, way better.'

'In a way. It's not *deus ex machina* or anything, because that liar Odin never turned me into a god, but it's *something*. Thought I might as well speed up the process a bit.'

'What process?'

It would appear I've completely accepted that I stabbed

my eye out, healed from it, and am talking to a floating head that knows... *Odin?* Whatever part of my brain whose job it is to police my reasoning has clearly taken the day off.

'The process of you figuring out what happened, and why I'm here. On that note: I'm Mimir – as I've said like three times now – and I'm the wisdom guy in the Norse myths. Except they're not really myths – or are they? I'm kidding; no one knows. Anyway, one of your eyes has recently been rent from your head, and that's kind of my calling card.'

'You stabbed out my eye?'

'Oh, no. That was all you. But in cases of lost eyeballs and deficiencies in the realm of wisdom, I sort of just... appear. While you took your little catnap, I've been trying to figure out how I can help.'

It might be the pills I swallowed, or the blood loss, or both, but none of what he's saying stands out as particularly weird to me. Like, sure, why can't Norse mythology be real and why shouldn't I have stabbed my own eyeball out and be talking to a disembodied floating head?

Mimir appears to sense some recognition.

'Good, you're getting it. So, what do you want me to do? Tell me your story and allow me to prescribe my genius.'

'I don't see how my story would be interesting, much less relevant to talk about now. Um, so what should I do now? Sounds like you and your genius have experience with the recently left eyeball-less.'

'Of course. First step is dealing with the wound, but somehow that doesn't appear to be an issue anymore', he says, pointing his nose down to the spherical mass of muscles and nerves over which he hovers. 'The bleeding, miraculously, seems to have stopped, and the gauze – along with the half a dozen antibiotics you swallowed – should help with preventing infection, so, well done. Now would probably be a good time, then, to let some people know that you're okay. Like Carol, perhaps.'

'How did you—'

'Your emails. Keep up. Lots to do.'

Leaving Mimir to hover behind me (or whatever he does if he isn't in my field of vision), I turn back to face my computer. Before checking and updating my email, I look to my clock to figure out how long I've been out. *Nine p.m.* – that's not so bad. Then I check the date. Two whole days have passed. Crap.

I return to my inbox, expecting very worried emails and missed calls from Carol and her assistant.

Carol has asked me to check in and see if everything's alright. Please contact anyone on the team as soon as this reaches you.

-Georgina

You alive?

-C

I'm touched. Almost moved to tears as I am, I reply with an equal amount of enthusiasm to each.

Dear Georgina,

Please let Carol and everyone else know that I am fine now – rehydrated meatloaf really didn't agree with me; I was violently sick and too weak to move from my bed until now. Please extend my deepest apologies if I have caused any distress.

Best,

Sam

To Carol:
Alive.
-*S*

Thirty seconds later, a reply comes in.
K. Good.
-*C*

She shouldn't have.

'Well, that part appears to be sorted.'

I would jump if I had the energy. Mimir is floating above my left shoulder, assessing the screen and then me.

'What's next on the list? Parents?'

'No, they aren't expecting to hear from me for a few days at least.'

'Then what, work? What is it exactly that you do? I must say, it doesn't seem as though you're very well suited to a job in the cold. In my day, you had to be. If you weren't, you were dead. But I digress.'

I'm starting to get really sick of this talking head. I don't care if he's real or in my mind – he's got to go. I make that as clear as I can. With my sense of reason finally returning, the frustration of having company – and chatty company at that – is starting to set in.

'I don't know, Mimir, isn't that your job, figuring out what I need? If you're so wise, hurry this all up and just give me some of that wisdom already or piss off. I'm fine now, no thanks to you, and I'm quite content to return to the way things were.'

Mimir furrows his grey brow and looks at me quizzically. The god – or paragon, as he put it – of wisdom doesn't seem used to this kind of reaction. But I'm not one for veneration, or time-wasting, so I'm more than ready for him to leave.

'Um. Is there – are you sure there isn't anything I can help you with?'

'No. I've had a pretty tough forty-eight hours, and your questions are probably the last thing I want to deal with right now. If you really want to make yourself useful, you can clean up the blood, but I think I'd prefer you left.'

I'm angrier than I thought I'd be. Not at any one thing in particular, I don't think, but enough things have lumped together in my brain to switch me from feeling overwhelmed to frustrated to angry. It's a progression I'm quite used to. Apparently, it's an effective deterrent, too, because before I have time to really register it, Mimir is gone.

It wasn't in a puff of smoke or anything. I actually don't know what I was expecting. Should I have been expecting something?

'No,' I say to myself.

Excessive blood loss caused a hallucination. I'm not going to start believing I actually saw some B-list Norse deity just because my brain made some faulty connections. Then again, if he was real, I am completely content not to see him or his ilk again.

My problems are mine and mine alone to solve, and he was proving more of a problem than a solution. He had to go. It all seems a bit abrupt, but very little of what just happened makes any sense at all, so I'm happy to move on.

I'm not some character in a myth or story that needs literal divine intervention. In fact, most of those characters that got such interventions would have been way better off without them.

Anyway, I've got a job to do. I take a look around my one big room. Right now, unfortunately, that job is cleaning up my blood and disembodied eyeball. Oh, joy. At least I've got a good story for whenever my relief team comes. *Don't piss off leopard seals – they're vicious*, I'll say. I smile and grab a mop.

Arthur & Pantheons

The process of categorisation is as old as men,

yet as old as man alone,

for no other animal species

categorises itself so neatly.

– Joshua Krook

WHEN I DECIDED to write about the system of divine pantheons in mythology, I'll admit the stories that make up the Arthurian canon were not examples that I had in mind.

What I pictured, as I imagine most would, were the Olympian gods of Greece, the wonderfully varied deities of Hinduism, and the Æsir and Vanir pantheons of gods of the Norse myths. True, most would be hesitant to even refer to Arthur as a figure of mythology, but I think exploring the concept of collections of gods or figures of import in mythology and folklore would benefit from a different perspective.

In many ways, the pantheon of Arthurian legend is a microcosm of the various pagan pantheons that existed prior to the rise of Christianity. The tales of King Arthur and his knights of the Round Table are full of religious and mythological allegories.

The existence of the Holy Grail has sparked comparisons to the magic drinking horn of Bran or Tuatha Dé Danann from Welsh and Irish mythologies respectively. The legends even have their roots in pagan mythology, with the figure of Arthur being based on a Celtic god of war, some scholars argue.

The Arthurian pantheon is a fascinating blend of different cultures and beliefs, and it is this diversity that makes the legends so rich and compelling. The various gods and goddesses represent different aspects of the human experience and psyche, and they come together to form a complete picture of the human condition.

From the love and beauty of the Lady of the Lake to the wisdom and strength of Merlin to the courage and valour of King Arthur himself, the pantheon of Arthurian legend has something for everyone.

It is also a reminder of the power of storytelling. The stories of the Arthurian pantheon have been passed down through the centuries, and they continue to inspire new generations of storytellers – musicals like Lerner and Loewe's *Camelot* and films like *Excalibur* and *Monty Python and the Holy Grail* come to mind as notable examples. The pantheon is a living testament to the power of myth and legend.

So, to the subject at hand – what is a pantheon? A pantheon is simply a group or collection of gods and goddesses. In the context of Arthurian legend, it refers to the various figures of power that appear in the stories. These figures can be deities from different cultures, or they can be mortals who have been elevated to a position of importance in the stories.

The pantheon that a society worships can say a lot about the values and beliefs of its people and their culture. For example, those focused on natural phenomena may place higher importance on the environment, while other cultures that focus on human experience may place higher importance on relationships and human interactions.

The basic story of King Arthur and his knights of the Round Table is that Arthur is a young man who inherits the throne of Britain from his father, Uther Pendragon. He then sets out to build a strong and just kingdom and, to that end, he gathers a group of noble knights to serve him. Together, they go on many adventures, and fight against evil forces that threaten the kingdom. Along the way, Arthur falls in love with the beautiful queen, Guinevere, and learns the hard lessons of what it takes to be a good leader.

With that context in mind, it becomes clear that the legend leans more toward discussions of human experiences and dynamics. Contrasting this with the beings of the Greek or Egyptian pantheons, the one key difference that stands out is their purpose. The characters that make up the legends of Arthur aren't to be worshipped or feared, nor do they exist as quasi-religious justifications for natural phenomena, but as figures to be revered, admired and, perhaps, copied.

In stories about a magical sword and wizard and sorceress, there is only so much suspension of disbelief to be had, but I would argue that the power and contemporary relatability of the legends come from their inherent humanity. The figure of a medieval king and his knights was an easily recognisable one, and allowed for – within that suspension of disbelief – a higher level of appreciation by an audience, in which they could see themselves within that story, if only in the periphery.

Pantheons are collective representations of the larger needs of a society. They reflect the culture, the moral standards and humanity within a community. A pantheon is a general term that refers to a group of different, conflicting figures – gods or heroes.

Arthurian legend deal generally with heroes so offers

a perspective into the nature of public consciousness at the time. It is aspirational for its audience and setting, and universally communicative of the themes of justice and heroism and adventure. Like all good myths, it's still a good story. And like all good stories, it keeps on giving.

My Brain on People

Anxiety is the dizziness of freedom.

– Søren Kierkegaard

ASTRID'S WALLS WERE empty. She needed to fix that. She *wanted* to, more like, but it felt closer to a need. Five feet to her right, Izzy's side of the room was a patchwork of kitschy décor. Fairy lights draped across the ceiling, casting a soft yellow glow on the Polaroids thumbtacked to the wall above her bed.

The lights ended behind her bedpost, the bed itself adorned with throw pillows and stuffed animals and a still-open half-empty suitcase. Lectures didn't start for another day, but even Izzy's desk was already heavily populated with colourful stationery, all neatly arranged.

Astrid's section was positively spartan in comparison. The walls were empty, as were her bed and desk. No lights hung from anywhere, and the duvet was an inoffensive eggshell. Everything she had brought with her fit neatly in the cupboard at the foot of the bed, save for her laptop, pen and pad of paper, which had been stuffed into a faded print tote bag that hung on the side of her chair.

Even the windows above each of their desks seemed different. The early evening light that streamed into the room seemed golden as it settled on Izzy's bed. Astrid got a dull, overcast light that only accentuated the starkness of her side of the room. It was like comparing a Scandinavian prison cell to a spoiled thirteen-year-old's bedroom.

As Astrid stared blankly at the adornment across from

her, the door to the room opened with an unsatisfying squeak and her roommate walked in, two girls trailing behind her.

They wore fashionable clothes, even on a day ostensibly for moving in, and had what looked like recently applied makeup. Tasteful, of course. With the exception of Jo, whose hair was almost comically red, the girls had perfectly styled auburn hair. Astrid's self-consciousness skyrocketed. She was much more simply dressed. She wore jeans and an oversized tee, and her blonde hair was done up in a messy bun. Astrid hadn't thought to make an effort on her appearance, and she felt the weight of that non-choice now.

'Oh, I thought you'd be out for dinner,' said Izzy, her hopeful subtext clear to Astrid. 'Anyway, these are my friends, Jo and Poppy.'

They both smiled kindly enough, but Astrid could feel them appraising her popularity or coolness, and she doubted they were impressed.

'Hi,' she said quietly.

Izzy continued, 'You don't mind if we stay here and play some music, do you?'

'No, no, of course not.'

Astrid smiled softly and tried not to look too desperate as the girls sprawled out on the bed, amongst the stuffed toys. She knew she couldn't go back to staring at the wall, so reached into her bag and pulled out a book. More of a prop than reading material in that moment, Astrid opened it near to the end and perused it thoughtfully. The girls didn't even look in her direction.

They were on their phones, and even though Astrid was

hopelessly addicted to her own, she felt a drop of superiority in a sea of self-consciousness for the fact that she was reading. She wasn't really reading, but they didn't need to know that. The book was Rudolf Simek's *Dictionary of Northern Mythology*, and it was required of all students of ancient folklore, but it wasn't what one would call a gripping read. Still, the entry about Tyr, Æsir god of war, distracted Astrid for long enough to realise she was hungry. She left the dorm room quickly but calmly, thinking as little as she could manage about the potentially judgemental sentiments being shared about her inside.

Food. She would find food.

* * *

Walking down the corridor of her dorm building, Astrid felt alone. Less than eight hours had passed since her arrival and things were already not going at all as she had expected. Astrid had hoped that in this new environment she would magically be a better version of herself. Going to university is a big deal, after all. She pushed the frosted glass door open and stepped into the cold.

It was early afternoon on possibly the busiest day on a university calendar, and the streets were virtually empty. Astrid spotted the last of the stragglers arriving and heaving cases out of car trunks, but was generally struck by the otherwise inactivity.

She considered for a moment going back inside, just because that's where everyone else was, but finally realised the futility of that act. Besides, she was still hungry, and there was bound to be a place or two to eat in her new home of Central London. Astrid laughed softly to herself and set off down the street, turning left.

The sky was edging into darkness and the city felt more awake than ever. The more she walked, the more she was pleasantly surprised to see crowded streets, bustling restaurants, queues outside theatres and old couples meandering in their freshly dusted-off winter coats.

Astrid found comfort in crowds like these. They lent a general sense of approval and seemed to cast an assuring blanket. She found a trendy fast-food place that wasn't too packed and punched her order into a greasy screen. Once she had collected her food, she claimed a booth to herself and enjoyed the feeling of independent company.

* * *

Astrid spent the next hour walking – she was in no hurry to get back to her room. Her side of it had no character, and Izzy's had three judgemental ones. Astrid just walked; no destination in mind, content in the action itself. She walked the length of Tottenham Court Road, past game shops and supermarkets and chain restaurants.

At the junction for Euston, she headed back in the direction of her new home. It took her down Gower Street which she found quieter, and far more lovely. It seemed to act, she thought, like a barrier, an unofficial demarcation between London in its consumerist glory and the pocket of old buildings and universities into which the students had begun their yearly swarm. There was still a sense of other-ism in the way Astrid thought about those students.

Despite the months of planning and preparation and excitement to prove the contrary, Astrid didn't fully think of herself as a student. She felt as though she'd been dropped into a world everyone else had been taught how to navigate, but she wasn't really concerned with playing along. And this was only her first day.

She eventually made it back to the dorm building, passively trying to connect – a friendly smile here, a little wave there – to the other students, who seemed to have settled in well. Astrid didn't have much faith in her 'efforts' to connect up to and including that point, but through small acts like these a lukewarm defence can be offered to her subconscious: that she had indeed tried… to an extent. Any friendships or connections that came of that effort were great; any failures were expected and not taken to heart.

Astrid walked past the small kitchen in their corridor, noticing Izzy, Poppy and Jo, along with two guys she had seen earlier that day. They were in varying stages of drunkenness, and crushed cider cans piled in and around the bin in the corner. Astrid made brief eye contact with Izzy, reading nothing in her expression, and kept walking.

Back in her room, Astrid took out her laptop and relaxed on her bed. She went through, for the tenth time, all of the timetables and documents and reading she would have to consult tomorrow, making sure they were all there – she knew they were.

Astrid could hear packs of new friends tumbling down the halls. The girls in their heels, their inaugural glamorous outfits of the year, the guys talking loudly about things Astrid was certain were of no interest to the girls. She was generalising and she knew it, but anything less and she was certain that she would have to consider joining them. Her current train of thought saved her from that prospect, one she found legitimately frightening. Besides, she rationalised, she would definitely have the chance to meet people in classes tomorrow.

To cement this point to her peers and herself, Astrid changed into her pyjamas and got ready for bed, walking amongst the soon-to-be inebriated masses as she went to the shared bathroom to brush her teeth. It was a small act of defiance. In her mind, it communicated a clear message: *I don't care that I'm not one of you. This is a choice, and not something I am ashamed of.*

But, like most sentiments one encounters at university, it was a lie. How she was being perceived was all Astrid thought about. The longer she did, the more the smallest, most innocuous moments and exchanges seemed to verge on apocalyptic.

As the images flashed through her mind, Astrid tried to reconcile the part of her that fixated on the minute, and the part of her that wanted not to want any of it. It was an internal battle of wills, and, as an example of her first twelve hours at university, it didn't inspire her with any confidence for the next three years.

See, the same part of her brain that fixated extrapolated,

too. It cherry-picked the least flattering moments of that day, exacerbating the emotions attached, and conjuring a 'likely' future based on those 'facts'.

Astrid was not aware of all the inner machinations of her mind, as no reasonable person can be expected to be. There was, however, something – someone, perhaps – out there who understood it all. Their epic destiny would soon converge with Astrid, new university student, aged eighteen.

* * *

It was the kind of shop that's been described a thousand times before with clichés that proved their worth. Indeed, it was dark, and the dust catching the rays of light from its tinted windows was the only source of illumination.

So, too, was it true that the cramped rooms seemed even smaller than they were as the customers squeezed through shelves of artefacts and curios, mystic-looking memorabilia and centuries-old furniture. It had the typically mysterious owner, half in shadow, though Astrid had not encountered him yet.

Between spending more time in the dorms or waiting on campus for her first lecture to start later that morning, Astrid instead opted to do some exploring. She steered clear of the side streets laden with students clustered together, holding coffees to go or smoking cigarettes. They were not the same comforting crowd as she'd encountered last night, they were each a potential threat. The vicinity around the mysterious shop, thankfully, was empty.

Astrid walked in and flinched a bit at the bell that marked her entrance. She browsed carefully the seemingly random collection of things that were for sale. She passed models of ships, and statues of various figures; a familiar snake swallowing its own tail, cast in what looked like bronze sat next to a clay elephant. The oddities continued for rooms without end, and just as Astrid had turned to leave, sufficiently creeped out, she heard a voice.

'Oh, hiya! I didn't hear you come in, I'm listening to an audiobook about marketing and I just got completely lost in it! Welcome to the shop.'

Astrid spun around, looking for the body to match the voice. There was a brief scuffle of footsteps and a figure stepped out of a doorway to her left. The man was tall, with curly black hair and eyes that seemed far too large for his thin face. He wore a black-and-white horizontally striped t-shirt, dark trousers, and a huge grin. A pair of earbuds stuck out of his right pocket.

'Looking for anything in particular? Or just—'

'I should get going. My lectures start soon, and I don't want to miss my first one,' Astrid said, already halfway towards the door. She nearly knocked over a pile of stuffed toys as she was leaving.

There was something about this place, something strange and familiar, something she was in no mood to figure out; she had enough on her mind already. The shopkeeper gave her a friendly nod.

'See you later,' he said.

Astrid barely heard him as she pushed open the door and stumbled back into daylight.

* * *

The morning had worn on, and she would have to hurry to get to campus. Astrid had walked quite a distance to escape the throng of students and had less time than she would have preferred to make the same journey back.

Astrid's first lecture of the day was 'Myths and Folklore in Context'. In the early afternoon, she had an introduction to the English Literature course, but the former was what she had been looking forward to. She had studied the campus map and made a beeline to her lecture hall. It was due to start at half past eleven, which gave her only a handful of minutes.

She burst in through the doors, a few seconds late. There were fifteen people sitting at desks, staring at her. It wasn't that many, but the course was not a popular one, and she estimated this was most of the class. The professor, a thirty-something man in a blue shirt and grey cardigan, gave her a kind smile.

As Astrid settled in the second row, she noticed two seats to her left one of Izzy's friends from last night, Jo. She smiled when she saw Astrid, but it didn't look friendly to her. Astrid barely listened to the professor (he introduced himself as Professor Abbott) and his opening spiel. Jo was a tether to a version of Astrid she had wanted to set aside when she was on campus.

'This is a fun course, but it's a lot of hard work, too, so I hope you guys are up for a challenge. We'll spend two weeks at a time homing in on a specific place and context, and looking at the myths and folklore that came out of it. The first week will be an introduction to the Greek myths, in case you are not already familiar. After that is Norse, and then Japanese, but I'll post the syllabus later today. At the end of the term, we'll spend a week comparing everything we've studied, and you will hopefully have a solid understanding of the pitch for the course.'

Jo was taking copious amounts of notes. Astrid was paying attention to the professor, but the majority of her brainpower was going towards trying to understand what Jo being in her class meant for her. The self-consciousness fixation was something Astrid had really hoped wouldn't be an issue once in an actual learning environment. As usual, though, something went differently from how she expected, and as usual, Astrid didn't know how to handle it.

'You should all have your dictionaries. Simek was meticulous in his research around this area and you'll find that book very useful, especially in terms two and three.'

Astrid looked for any reaction from Jo. Nothing. Maybe she hadn't seen her 'reading' it last night. Astrid didn't know what Jo thought, which was perhaps even more annoying. No clear-cut answer – no mockery, no sign of derision or haughtiness. Astrid hadn't expected her dorm life to affect her academics, but equally, hadn't expected the reverse to be true as well. She would have to work really hard to separate the two, because Astrid had already deemed one beyond reproach for her, and she didn't like the idea of what would happen if she let them coalesce into one.

Astrid knew she was reading too much into Jo's presence, but that didn't make it any easier. When the lecture ended,

Astrid was one of the first out of the door, desperate, at that point, for a change of scene.

* * *

The English Lit lecture was packed. Possibly the most subscribed-to course, and Astrid felt fine sitting in the middle of that crowded lecture hall. She was tired already of thinking about why she wasn't nervous around the dozens and dozens of students, many of whom she had avoided on the street that morning. She didn't want to keep psychoanalysing herself because it took effort away from actually socialising, and there was no way to evaluate whether her conclusions were true.

In this case, though, the answer was simple. There was no attention on her. Astrid was one of around two hundred students, each no more remarkable than the other, each focusing on the professor pacing at the front of the room.

As in her previous lecture, she was paying attention, but her brain was still focused on processing everything else. Her hands typed notes she would worry about understanding later.

Okay, she thought. *Let's make a quick assessment.* Like Astrid had done a thousand times before, she recounted her situation to herself, taking stock of what had been going on.

I got to the dorm yesterday, late morning. I said bye to Dad and spent the afternoon unpacking. I met my roommate, Izzy, whose side of the room is covered in decorations. She's more popular than me, I can feel it. Izzy brought two girls over – her friends, she said. How had she made friends that quickly? She arrived an hour after I did! The friends acted nice, but I could feel them judging me, so I had to get out of there soon after I met them. I ate a quick dinner and walked for a bit, which was really nice. Actually, it's the only time I've felt calm since I got here (a day ago).

Then there was that shop this morning – I want to go back there but can't tell why. Jo being in my class for the Intro to Myths lecture really threw me. I'd already decided to not try socially at the dorms, but now I feel like I'm losing my shot to meet people at the school. Two things I expected to be separate aren't. You know what, I am going to try at the dorms. I got off to a crap start and maybe that will help put things back where they should be. I'm going to start with Izzy – go big or go home, right?

'Right. Any questions?'

A few hands went up. The professor had finished talking, and Astrid emerged from her thoughts. She looked down at her notes – she had written everything she had heard the professor say, verbatim. Before Astrid had time to think about the coolness of that fact, the person to her left tapped her arm.

'Hey, are you okay?'

It was a guy wearing a red hoodie and a pair of jeans. He had shaggy brown hair and soft features, and his expression was a mix of concern and amusement. She might have thought he was cute if she wasn't completely surprised.

'Huh? Yeah, why?'

'Oh, it's just that you were typing for like thirty minutes non-stop and suddenly stopped really abruptly. Wanted to make sure your brain was still working.'

He spoke in a loud whisper, but no one was paying either of them any attention – why would they?

'I'm fine. I guess I was just kinda distracted.'

'Okay. Good to know everything's working up there'. He tapped his temple and smiled. 'We wouldn't want anyone going down on the first day.'

'Yeah, thanks.'

Astrid felt really unprepared. This random guy was giving her some attention and she didn't want to waste it, but she had no idea what to say next. Thankfully, he had that covered, too.

'I'm Max, what's your name?'

She looked around again, searching for anyone that might be judging her. 'Astrid,' she said finally, hoping she hadn't paused for too long.

'Nice. Cool. Cool. Do you wanna maybe exchange Insta handles? It'd be nice to know some people on this course. Only if you want to – totally cool if not.'

'Yeah, sure,' she said, and Max immediately wrote his down on a corner of paper, tore it off, and gave it to her.

He had a nervous energy that oddly calmed Astrid down a bit. It was as if knowing that someone else was actually *trying* in a conversation took some of the pressure off her.

There was a short lull, so Astrid decided to try and fill it.

'So are you studying any other—'

At that moment, two hundred students stood up to leave, and the room was filled with a loud hum. The professor had stopped talking, and questions had been answered.

Max smiled apologetically and said, 'Well, it was nice to

meet you,' before joining the exodus.

Astrid had opened her mouth to say, *Yeah, you too*, but the little sound her voice made was quickly drowned out.

Outside the building, Astrid made her way to the forum. Clusters of students that had met no more than a day ago were dotted around a large courtyard space. Some sat on the brick steps, others laughed in between puffs on their vapes. As usual, and as she had expected she would be, Astrid was uncomfortable. She didn't like how comfortable everyone seemed to be and with such little effort – it was unfair. She was *jealous*. It was like learning a language; to the people on the inside it looked effortless and useful, while all the learner saw was exclusion and a challenge.

Astrid noticed Max chatting to some other people she had seen in the English Literature lecture. He was bouncing on the balls of his feet, clearly that nervous energy hadn't left him just yet. Or maybe it was just the cold. Astrid considered going up to the little group he was in and introducing herself, but quickly dismissed the idea.

Meeting someone at all was a win, and she didn't want to ruin that small streak with the possibility of something going wrong in a group interaction. Keep it simple, build up to it slowly. She was fully aware that her 'success' was thanks to an initiative that Max took, but a part of her brain didn't play up that fact, allowing her a small moment of triumph over her failed expectations that had made the last day so stressful.

Astrid walked past Max's cluster and made brief eye contact, trying for a nonchalant smile. He returned it, filling her with a taste of that triumph again, and she set off back to the dorm.

* * *

Astrid spent an hour clarifying anything academic that she hadn't processed on campus. Her empty desk quickly filled up with sheets of paper, outlining essay ideas and syllabuses and reading lists and deadlines for the next term, which some unconscious part of her had helpfully kept track of.

Late afternoon was spilling into evening when Izzy got back to the room, the dim gloom of her phone reflected in her eyes. In a tote bag of her own, she carried a box of multicoloured pens and a thick pad of note paper, both of which looked unused. She tossed the bag next to her chair and slumped onto her bed, her attention never wavering away from her phone.

'Hey,' Astrid said. She was trying for the first time to actually connect with her roommate.

'Hey,' Izzy replied noncommittally.

Astrid left it there. She didn't want to push it and make too much of an impression, especially not a bad one. At the same time, she didn't feel the same judgement coming from Izzy that she had when Jo and Poppy were around, which made Astrid more hopeful than she thought wise.

Having finished all of the work she had, and spurred on by that hope, Astrid added Max on Instagram and accepted his own request. Acting faster than her self-doubt, she sent him a DM saying hi and promptly threw her phone onto her bed. It gave her a second to process what she'd just done without having to stare at and second-guess it.

Astrid took a quick, deep breath to calm herself down, and cleaned up the mess that had accrued on and around her desk. She pulled out folders and files she had stuffed into her desk drawers the day before and created a pocket of order in the chaos.

She didn't really have anything else to do after that. Izzy was still on her phone and had barely moved for half an hour, and Astrid felt weird being inactive around her; she didn't want it to come across that she was staring at Izzy or being weird.

Fortunately, Astrid's body reminded her how long it had been since she last ate, once again giving her something to do. She considered inviting Izzy out to grab a bite but decided against it for now. The possibility of a 'no' was pressure she didn't need.

Twice in twenty-four hours, Astrid had walked out of this building eager to get out, but it was different this time. Not markedly so, but enough to be meaningful to her. She was running on hope. Not sustainably, but contentedly.

Once again in the chilling air, Astrid felt refreshed. She headed in the direction of the fast-food place she had visited last night, happy to be encouraging some consistency. An annoyingly prudent voice within her, however, reminded her that she was on a budget, and that she had bought cooking supplies that should see some use sooner or later.

She made no effort to take the quickest route to the supermarket. Astrid walked around and took in her new neighbourhood, and eventually found herself outside that strange shop she had fled from that morning. Something about it had drawn her in for a second time.

Again, Astrid found herself in and amongst piles and stacks and collections of antiques and memorabilia. It was such a wild variety, the only real ties between any of the objects was the randomness that they all inhabited. This time, the owner (Astrid assumed) was within view as soon as she entered.

'Hello, again,' he said, seemingly pleased and strangely unsurprised that she had returned after her hasty exit.

'Hi.'

'My name's Don, and I'm going to help you find exactly what you need.'

'What?'

'Sorry, I tend to get straight down to brass tacks too quickly, I've heard it before. So, welcome to my shop! It's a bit of an institution in these parts. I specialise in curios and the curious, and you seem to be the latter. Now, something in here is calling to you, I can feel it. But what is it…?'

Astrid said nothing. She didn't know what to say – she was utterly confused by what was going on. Don started walking deeper into the store, muttering to himself, and Astrid was surprised to see herself following him.

The shop was even eerier in the evening. The disappearing sun cast long, obscuring shadows. Every couple of metres Don would stop, pick up an object, smell or lick it, and walk away shaking his head.

'Not metal,' she heard him say to himself. 'The amulet, maybe? No, no.'

This went on for a few minutes, and eventually Astrid found herself less taken with this whole idea, and once again quite keen to leave.

'Um, I think I'm going to go now. Thanks for, uh, thanks for trying to help, I guess.' She spoke softly but got his attention.

Astrid wound through the rooms, back the way she came. Again, she felt a weird pull to this place, but the amount she was getting creeped out was more than enough to supersede that fact. She neared the door, for what she hoped was the last time, before hearing Don call out.

'Wait! Wait, I've got it!'

Astrid stopped and turned. He was hurrying out of the rooms and had a relieved grin on his face.

'I can't believe I missed it. Of course it was here!'

He gestured towards the pile of stuffed toys Astrid had nearly knocked over that morning. He picked one up from the bottom of the pile and handed it to her. It was in the shape of a head and about as big as a melon, with deeply tanned 'skin' and a large brown beard. That pull within her felt stronger than ever.

Astrid stared at it for a good ten seconds, before remembering that she was in a shop.

'Um, how much is it?'

'I'd let him go for two goat horns, or five quid, whichever you've got on you.' He smiled, like he'd told a joke only he understood.

Astrid paid him his money and left, still confused by the whole interaction but more intrigued by the odd souvenir she'd just picked up. It was her first piece of decoration at the very least, she supposed.

At the supermarket, she stuffed the toy in her left coat pocket. It created a noticeable bulge at her side, but less noticeable, she reasoned, than if she'd held it in her hand as she walked around. Besides, this was an impromptu visit, and she hadn't brought a bag.

Astrid pondered the strange interaction she'd just had in that shop while she wandered the aisles. It was mainly the shopkeeper that confused her. The shop itself, with its antiques and trinkets, was similar to the types she had visited with her dad a dozen times before, but its owner seemed too aware of her. That's the only way she could describe it to herself. Don wasn't a problem, she didn't think. Astrid had no idea *what* he was.

She picked up some easy-to-cook food: pasta, prepped salads and other low-effort meals. Astrid could cook basic meals – nothing fancy – but right now she was trying to compromise between ease of preparation, taste and cost. She was willing to sacrifice the middle one, she decided, and added plenty more reasonably priced, filling foods. Into the cart went some new potatoes, rice, readymade sauces and some hummus.

Hummus – a wise choice. It goes well with a nice Chardonnay, said a voice in her head. But it wasn't hers.

Astrid knew that for a fact, but also knew that her mind was still reeling from Don and his shop, so didn't give it any more thought. She chose the last of her things, paid, and stepped into the London evening.

* * *

Back at the dorms, Astrid stashed the toy under a pillow in her room before making her way downstairs into the kitchen to put away her haul.

The kitchen was a large open-plan space that took up the entire basement level. There were about a dozen kitchen suites along the perimeter, and clusters of seats and tables occupying the middle. A handful of groups sat and enjoyed their own meals. As she unpacked, Astrid looked at them wistfully.

They looked so at ease, comfortable in each other's presence. Astrid wanted that so desperately, and right now, it still felt unattainable. It was the type of fear and anxiety that convinced her there was nothing to be afraid of until she was presented with what she wanted. It was a cruel trick she played on herself.

In this case, there wasn't anything Astrid believed she would realistically do, so she went about cooking her meal, trying not to think about that. She made the pasta and a simple sauce – it required little effort and little cleaning up. After a while, her quietness and the quietness of her immediate surroundings, contrasted with the drone of conversation elsewhere in the room, became harder to ignore.

As she ate her pasta, she fished in her pocket for a tangled heap of earphones and put them on, queuing up music on her phone. It seemed predetermined that her time alone would be spent feeling forlorn, but she considered this an effort to regain some control over that time. Not to mention the extra barrier it put up between her and expected social interaction.

Astrid ate and washed up quickly, in no mood to spend more time in the kitchen than necessary. She kept her earphones in as she walked out, and when she passed the group of friends closest to the door, she made eye contact with one, smiled, and continued on.

Back in her room, Astrid peeled back her duvet and retrieved the toy from under the pillow, setting it on her desk. It toppled over, so she stood it up against a pile of books to her right. An odd sense of calmness washed through her mind, counterintuitively jarring in its immediacy.

Before the calm, Astrid had had a lot going through her mind. Jo was in the room with Izzy, and for reasons Astrid couldn't articulate even to herself, Jo's presence bothered her.

Nevertheless, Astrid used her newfound mental clarity to get her things ready for tomorrow. She only had one commitment, her first English seminar, and even though she preferred the folklore subject on the whole, she was looking forward to having something to focus on. Also, the possibility of seeing Max again felt exciting, and there was only a little nervousness attached to that feeling. He had replied 'hi' to her own message, which wasn't a lot, but the digital attention made her happy nonetheless.

Izzy and Jo paid Astrid no mind, and the reverse was true as well. But it wasn't an attempt on Astrid's part to appear nonchalant, she was legitimately uninterested in dedicating too much mental bandwidth to obsessing. She didn't know where the change in her outlook had come from, nor did she care; Astrid was just happy to be unabashedly happy.

She kept to herself the rest of the evening. Fewer people went out compared to last night, at least based on the reduced cacophony in the corridor. Astrid just lay in bed and set out to watch something. She would normally have put on a movie, or one of her comfort shows, but tonight her first choice was a reality show about drinking. She thought nothing of it.

* * *

The next morning, Astrid woke up earlier than she had planned. After a quick meal of some sugary breakfast cereal, she decided to go for a walk – it was barely seven a.m., and her seminar wasn't until noon.

There was a light drizzle outside, but she didn't mind. She put on a jacket and set out. Any other heat she needed, Astrid joked to herself, her brain would produce for her. Working as intensely as it did for her overthinking, Astrid reasoned it dealt with the stress similarly to a computer, with an output of hot air.

Except none of that came. She turned down Seven Dials, though in a state of mental ease Astrid still wasn't quite used to. It was nice, of course, but unusual. Her walks were the periods of time specifically allocated to her overthinking, the practised repetition that soothed her as her mind tried to manage the weight of its own concern. Even though she noticed it, she wasn't even fixating on that unusualness.

In this newfound state, Astrid was not free from thought, just the burden that it usually placed upon her. She considered the stakes of decisions and choices – about her social life and study – but did not feel the power of each in turn. In an image of her mind, she pinched and zoomed out, shifting her perspective from a foot soldier in a singular fight to a general, before whom lays the entire battleground.

Astrid spent her whole walk past Trafalgar Square and along Northumberland Avenue down to the river using her clarity to define her clarity. She estimated that she spent half her time in general just thinking about her own thinking.

It did eventually get repetitive. There are only so many conclusions we are able to glean about ourselves, after all. Crossing the river at Embankment, she turned her thoughts as best she could to the subject of her sociability. It was a common topic up in her brain, and the classics began to play. This time, though, with a new perspective.

As she walked, Astrid let those thoughts sink into her mind, somewhere she wouldn't have to focus on them. She let in only surface-level observations, content to experience the mundane.

It was still early, but there were a handful of pedestrians that had also thought a walk along the river would be a nice way to start the day. A woman in her early thirties jogged past, pushing a pram. An old man sat on a bench to Astrid's left, facing the water. A man barely older than her walked into a nearby coffee shop, a sullen look on his face. Operating that sacred coffee machine, his morning would be spent making others' better. That struck a chord with Astrid. Some part of her resonated with the idea of putting other people at ease at personal cost.

Her interlude from thought hadn't lasted long. But she

had conjured a ripe morsel of a notion that refused to go untasted. *Do I really do that? Try to put others at ease?* She smiled. The suggestion seemed almost comical – her social shortcomings were entirely self-centred. They had to be, that's the only way it made sense to her.

Not exactly, a voice played in her head. But once again, it wasn't hers. The voice didn't elaborate, and Astrid thought nothing more of it. She crossed the river on the Millennium Bridge and headed back in the direction of her new home. Up the steps to St Paul's Cathedral, around the side and onto Chancery Lane. Back in her thought-less state of mind, she just enjoyed the walk.

* * *

It was a few minutes past eleven when she got back. Astrid heard a small hum of people having a late breakfast in the kitchen, and Izzy was still asleep in their room. Astrid showered, got dressed and went through some materials for the upcoming English lecture. Izzy's alarm went off soon after that, a harsh tonal beep that elicited a guttural groan.

'Morning,' Astrid said.

'Mmmmmmmmph,' the roommate replied, covering her ears with her pillow. A few seconds later, she relented and turned off the alarm, sitting up a bit.

'What time is it?'

Astrid checked her phone. 'Uh, eleven-thirty. Got anything going on today?'

Izzy forced her eyes open and got up. 'I've got a lecture in like fifteen minutes.'

'Yeah, me too.'

Talking to Izzy didn't feel so difficult in that moment. Astrid didn't know why, but it seemed likely that she didn't expect to be judged by someone who still had sleep in their eyes. If only people were always rousing from sleep. Astrid didn't like how it sounded even to herself, but the dulled perceptions of others put her at ease.

In the time it had taken Astrid to think that, Izzy had gotten fully dressed in a long skirt and a simple blouse, and was now sitting in front of the vanity on her desk, lip gloss container in hand. Either Astrid had been staring blankly at a wall for five minutes, or Izzy was an impressively fast dresser.

'So, um, what's your lecture today about?' Astrid dared ask even though the risk of judgement had risen exponentially. She hoped she could trust her own judgement.

'Oh, I don't know. It's probably gonna be some basic chemistry lesson. Get everyone up to speed with the easy stuff – titration, chromatography, cell biology – you know?'

'Wait, what are you studying?'

'Biochem. Why?'

'I don't know, I just thought... I guess I was expecting something else.'

Astrid had forgotten how toxic her own judgement of others could be.

'Ha, I know. It's boring as hell but I'm good at it and jobs pay a ton so...' Izzy smacked her lips and turned to Astrid. 'What's three years, right?'

Just then, Poppy came into the room and asked Izzy if she

was ready to go. The pair left a few seconds later. Astrid tried to balance her feelings of happiness for a brief connection with Izzy, and her disappointment at her leaving so quickly, and the weight that simple act held over her.

Astrid gathered her laptop and books into her bag and left soon after them, mostly pleased with the encounter, and looking forward to another day on campus. Like Izzy, she was good at what she studied. But the difference was, she liked it.

There was a light flow of foot traffic between the dorms and campus. Pairs and threes and fours walked in line with each other, clutching books and folders to their chests, smiling and talking with ease.

Astrid walked behind them, occasionally overtaking if they were too slow. She didn't really give any one group or person her attention. Her thought process had changed for some inexplicable, beautiful reason. Now, the valuable space they took up in her mind had downgraded their presence to awareness. Astrid knew what they were all doing, but she didn't speculate. Sure, she wasn't yet proactive, but at least she was tamping down her reactions.

Astrid was almost late to her English seminar, but so was another half of the class. She was one of several dozen being bottlenecked through the double doors. As Astrid walked up the steps and into the seating area that sloped up another storey, she kept her eyes peeled for Max.

It suddenly occurred to Astrid that she may not even recognise him; he was one out of hundreds of faces, and she had seen him for maybe ten minutes in total. Would she even recognise him from a two-year-old picture on his Instagram page?

Thank God, she thought to herself. There he was, halfway up, in the same red hoodie. Then her heart sank. He was sitting and chatting to someone in the seat to his left – a girl – and there was already someone in the other seat next to him. Astrid was fumbling, looking for a place nearby to sit, when the girl laughed, touched his shoulder and moved a few rows down to what must have been her original spot.

As gracefully as she could manage, Astrid shuffled into the row, smiling with a tight lip and an unspoken apology in her eyes as she dodged the legs and bags of her classmates. She sat in the free seat, and said hi to Max. His attention was all she really wanted. He smiled as she sat down.

'Hi,' he said. 'How's the first week been treating you?'

Astrid started pulling books out of her bag, stacking them in front of her as she thought of a response.

'I've been trying to make sure I'm ahead of all my work. Haven't really met many people yet.'

She felt nervous saying as much. Though the judgements of random passers-by on the pavement were easily enough ignored, Astrid felt some immutable stakes with Max, like a house of cards she had sworn she would protect.

'That's a shame. At least you're going to understand the next two hours, though.'

And she did. A critical dissection of Defoe's work as it pertains to colonisation, boring as it may have been, made complete sense to Astrid. She knew the two main components of university were the work and the people, and she had resolved herself to never fail at the former. As a result, she had really stayed on top of her required reading. But, God, was Defoe boring.

At several points during the lecture, Max had to lean over to see what Astrid had written, which made her feel proud of her work in more ways than she had intended.

The lecture ended as undramatically as it had started, and Astrid walked alongside Max as he left, listening as he went on about the amount of reading they had to do.

'I wish I'd done more research about how much research I'd have to do on this course,' he said.

Astrid chuckled as they both stepped into the sun. Her eyes darted, almost instinctually, searching for the group she had seen Max talking to last time. She wasn't sure if she resented or was frightened by them. Before she had the chance to spiral even more, Max cut into her thoughts, catching her by surprise.

'Anyway, there's this small party happening at my dorm this weekend, you should come along if you'd like to.'

Giddy inside, Astrid tried to hide her excitement.

'Um, yeah, that sounds like fun.'

'Great! I'll send you the details later.'

Max walked off and Astrid stood there, in awe at her luck. Heading back home, Astrid had to contain the urge to skip.

* * *

The rest of the week passed in a blur. In and out of lectures and the dorm, Astrid kept herself busy. She spent her time walking and writing and reading about Ancient Greek belief systems and not feeling bad about herself. She passed Don's store again, and considered going in, but didn't know what she would even say. That doll had been a fantastic lucky charm.

Astrid saw Max once, and they made polite conversation. He did send her the details on Instagram – Saturday starting at nine. Izzy apparently noticed a shift in her mood. She spoke up as Astrid was getting ready for the party.

'You seem… I dunno, happier? Like, less panicky I guess.'

Astrid was more than happy to tell her why.

'Yeah, I've been invited to a party tonight,' Astrid said, trying to pick a dress from her wardrobe. Which dress should she choose, red or black?

'Ooh, nice. Can I come?'

Astrid was a bit taken aback, but in too good a mood to refuse.

'Yeah, I don't see why not.'

At that moment, Jo walked in. Izzy immediately piped up.

'Guess what, J? We're going to a party. Astrid here snagged herself an invitation and we're crashing it.'

Astrid was a bit flustered but sensed no malice in the words. Jo looked at her.

'Thanks for the invite. And go with the red one. It'll suit you better.'

'Um, cool,' Astrid said. 'No problem.'

Just like that, everything was looking up. Izzy went with Jo to help pick her outfit, and Astrid looked at the address for the eighth time that hour. As she was figuring out the best way to get there, she heard a voice.

'You're welcome,' it said.

Astrid spun, looking for the source. It sounded like it was coming from her desk.

'Um, hello?' she said softly. 'Who's there?'

It spoke again. This time, she was certain it had come from her desk – was it her doll, making the sound? Was that possible?

'I'd be offended if you weren't honouring me well tonight.'

'Who are you?'

The stuffed head seemed to sigh.

'Only the coolest god ever. Dionysus, in the fluff. I'm just here to give you some advice before the party.'

Astrid was still processing the whole *god* thing, but it – he? – went on.

'I've watched you give a truly appalling social performance this past week but fear not! All is not lost. For you have the master of making friends on your side! Quickly, before Izzy gets back, I need to tell you something.'

Astrid was quiet, still a bit stunned. Dionysus did not appear to notice. Then again, he was currently an inanimate object.

'My advice is simple. First: drink. It'll help a ton with any issues you have with people tonight. Second: don't give the people any more thought and effort than they're worth. But don't give them no effort at all. Embrace hedonism for one night and just try and unwind. I've given you a blessing – my presence – but you need all the help you can get. So don't stand in your own way.'

With the party god's parting words, Astrid felt… the

same. But she remembered what he had said, provided he wasn't a hallucination, and that gave her some comfort. Twenty minutes later, she left with the other two girls for her first university bacchanalia. The first of many, she knew. Not hoped, knew.

'This had better not mess with my schoolwork,' she said to herself, in case the god was listening to her. 'I refuse to fail.'

The Dark Blue Sky

As is a tale, so is life: not how long it is,

but how good it is, is what matters.

– Seneca

DALILA KAMEL PULLED the blanket over her grandfather's chest. He stirred, his head shifting slightly from side to side, his mouth curling into a disapproving frown.

'The spirits,' he had told her when she was a child, 'they are our dreams, little one, good and bad. They are not to be controlled, nor feared.'

But Dalila was terrified. Fear and doubt had been her prevailing emotions for years now, she had been given so much responsibility far too young. Nevertheless, she completed her ritual. She tidied the house, lit fresh candles in the places of hardened pools of wax, and completed the chores that were hers alone to do.

She washed her face in the shallow basin by the door, before walking to her grandfather's bedside.

'Good night, *jadiy*. See you in the morning.'

Dalila kissed her grandfather on the forehead and left for work.

* * *

At night, Dalila worked as a cook. Having been referred by friends of friends of friends, she had been working at the minister's house for almost two months now. She was barely eighteen, but had the air of someone a decade older.

It was, as always, a long night. The hours warped and stretched, threatening to go on forever as Dalila sat by the stove, heat and aroma coming for her from every direction. Pots of various sizes lined the stovetop, each with their own complementary concoction. She had learned early on that the minister was a man of habit, of routine. In some ways, it made her job easier, and she often found herself doing the work without even thinking about it.

For the most part, though, Dalila hated the routine. The repetitive monotony lulled her into a fatigued state, and the lack of any novelty really weighed down her mind.

Once done, she placed the food in the various serving vessels, each carved with ornate figures, humans with animals for heads. Dalila smiled briefly and packed up, leaving for home.

In the early hours of the morning, she loved to walk through the streets of her city – Alexandria. The oppressive heat and sound and smell that would settle like a fog as the day wore on were only in their early stages. Besides, few others were awake this early, so walking was all the more peaceful.

Dalila reached the door to her home. It was her parents' home, really, but they hadn't been around to use it since she was a child. She didn't know the truth, but she preferred her grandfather's lies, anyway. *They're off looking for a kingdom fit for their princess.* It was Dalila's, and her grandfather's, and she was happy with that now.

Stepping in, Dalila immediately felt the cooler air, waking her up just a little. Away from the sun and its light, heat had little place in their collection of three stone rooms.

Three years ago, in the early days of her cooking work, Dalila would have had to change from her dirty clothes into fresh ones with the little time she had before her real job started. She was, though, a much more skilful cook now, and had perfected the art perhaps not of cooking, but of keeping the food in pots and not on her clothes. Dalila spent the spare moments she had washing her face in the cool water once more and said goodbye to her grandfather again before leaving.

As she closed the door behind her, a sound struggled to reach her – the voice of her only remaining family.

'Good morning, Dalila,' replied Asim Kamel, 'my guide, my stars.'

* * *

It was barely light when she got to the House of Threads. An unassuming stone building, it was sacred to Dalila. Sounds had begun to fill in as the city woke up around her. As she entered her place of work, her place of passion, Dalila smiled. It was a warm smile, and one her manager, Sadiki, returned. The cooking she did to earn money for her grandfather, but this she did for herself.

Sadiki was a tall and heavyset man, somewhere in his early fifties, and beloved by all who knew him. His long, scruffy beard was matched by his equally untamed hair. He would joke that he'd had a full beard since he was a toddler, and Dalila could imagine it.

She stepped around the loose fabric on the floor to join him behind the counter. Sadiki immediately handed her a stack of messily folded clothes. He smiled apologetically, as if almost sorry he had to give her work.

'See you in a couple of hours,' she said, and disappeared into the back room.

Barely big enough for her to extend her arms in any direction, the back room, designated as Dalila's workspace, was tiny. She loved it. It was her own, it was the place she associated most with what she loved to do – sew.

Dalila sat down on her bench. It was a plank of light wood that Sadiki had fastened to the walls on either side with a few now-rusty nails. She lay the pile of clothes to one side at her feet, and settled in.

The work was straightforward, but by no means simple. Ever since Sadiki had given her the opportunity to practise her passion *and* get paid, Dalila knew she would give every stitch her all. Granted, the money wasn't much – just what he could spare at the end of each week, but Dalila was no less grateful. She adjusted waistband sizes for the self-conscious women of the neighbourhood, and patched holes in various items of clothing belonging to some extremely energetic children.

Dalila wasn't naturally talented or gifted with the work, but what she lacked in preternatural sewing ability and any negotiating skill, Sadiki had once told her, she surpassed in dedication to her craft. She was here every day. Dalila did the most basic work a thousand times over and got good at it. She developed her instinct – worked hard at it, trusted it, but still never relied upon it. She remained alert and focused for every hour she spent in that room; Dalila never took it for granted.

She loved what she did, and her nimble fingers created carefully choreographed work which reflected that – elegantly unpretentious.

In addition to the spare change she got at the House of Threads, Sadiki allowed her to take any spare material home, precious cloth that would otherwise see no use. She had never used it, and kept it all neatly folded in a small box beneath her grandfather's bed. Dalila dreamed, though, of what combined future she and it could make.

She always left work in good spirits, but it was never long before the exhaustion set in. Dalila had been awake for the better part of a day, and it was now, typically, when her body reminded her she had limits.

* * *

The sun was well into its downward trajectory by the time she got back home. She was ready to collapse – knowing that the next several hours would be difficult but she'd get through them, because she always did. As far as motivation went, though, it was a cold comfort. Dalila ate a simple meal of bread and tomato sauce, and sat by her grandfather's side to feed him the same before she could rest her eyes.

He ate a little, not entirely lucid. As she stored away the food, though, she heard a whisper.

'Dalila?' The sound took some time to form on her grandfather's lips.

She had scarcely heard him speak in days now. For a man usually so unable to keep quiet, this had worried Dalila, but only now was she reminded of it.

'*Jadiy*? Are you awake, are you okay?'

She sat on a stool by his bed and took his hand.

'How—' he let out a wheezy cough. 'How was work?'

Dalila smiled. Ever the worrier, her grandfather. She supposed she got it from him.

'Work was wonderful,' she said. He did not know of her long hours in the kitchen, the money she needed to earn there – he was barely able to open his eyes most of the day. She did not want to worry him more. Dalila told him often, though, of the sewing, of Sadiki. She loved expressing her passion to her grandfather.

'Do you have time,' he asked after a while, 'to entertain an old man with a story? I used to tell you so many when you were a child…' He trailed off.

Dalila smiled gently, though her brow furrowed slightly. She glanced back at the darkened sunlight spilling underneath the front door, knowing she only had so much time to rest. He sensed her hesitation.

'Never mind, child. You have another long day of work tomorrow.'

I have a long night of work in just a few hours, she thought. She wasn't angry or bitter, in fact she was ever so slightly amused. She took a deep breath, storing her fatigue deep within her, where it would doubtless return with accrued interest.

'Which story would you like? Hero or god, good or evil?'

'There are no such things. Would you tell me of the sky? I can hardly remember its shades of blue.'

The story of Nut, the sky goddess, was one lodged in her memory – it existed as far back as her memories went. She began, the words flowing out of her.

'In the days when the ground was black, and the river was home, there was a goddess people spoke of. Mistress of the sky, they called her. *Nut*.'

A small smile formed on her *jadiy*'s face, heartening Dalila.

'It was told that she had a love – the earth, Geb. They would be responsible for bringing into being the next greatest gods. Sure enough, Nut was soon pregnant, five children of divinity growing in her belly.'

'Something's going to go wrong,' her grandfather interjected, 'something always goes wrong.'

His eyes glinted with simple mischief. *Of course he knew something would go wrong – it was he who had taught her this story.* Dalila reflected his smile.

'Would my fine audience member care to take over? It's evident he's familiar with the tale and I should, as he said, get some rest.'

He slowly mimed zipping his lip with his fingers and gestured for her to continue.

'Something did, in fact, go wrong. The great god Ra, captain of the sun-boat, was jealous.'

'I knew it,' her grandfather whispered.

Dalila feigned a disapproving frown and went on.

'There are few things worse than the ire of a god, and Ra

was no minor god. He vowed that Nut would pay for her insolence. Now, though she was the goddess of the sky, she was no match for the sun-god. Nut was powerless to argue as Ra decreed that he would not let her give birth on any of the 360 days of the year. They were under his control, after all. But the old goddess was desperate and wasn't about to give in so easily.'

Dalila was hitting her stride. The details of the story swarmed in her mind, exactly as they had the first time she'd heard her grandfather retell them. A jealous god. A goddess, pleading, then resolute. Her *jadiy*'s eyes gleamed with happiness.

'Perhaps the greatest threat to gods and their plans is pure reason. As is often the case, forethought is an ability not many deities take advantage of. The notable exception, however, was Thoth, god of wisdom. Nut knew that if anyone could figure a way forward for her, it was Thoth. Luckily for her, she was right.'

'There is no luck in the story of the gods, Dalila. They are above it. Immune to it. Ra simply underestimated Nut.'

'Perhaps, *jadiy*. But you're skipping ahead.'

'My apologies.'

'As I was saying, Thoth had a plan. So, he called out to the moon. Khonsu abided. Tall and pale, he glowed with faint moonlight, and that was exactly what he was summoned for. Thoth reasoned that, if she could get enough moonlight from Khonsu, Nut could make some days of her own. They just needed to appeal to his inner gambler, and it didn't take long for him to pull out the dice. Nut and Thoth won—'

'Wait, you're not going to add any of the suspense? Sometimes I forget how young you are, how impatient. Do you not remember how I would tell this part – the dramatic pauses, the tension I built?'

Dalila had been enjoying telling the story and bringing the memories back to the surface of her mind. But she was tired, and no amount of fun she was having right now could hold that off forever. Her grandfather had seen through her little shortcut, though.

'Sorry, *jadiy*. I guess I don't have your skill with stories.'

'Bah! You're still young,' he said, though this time it didn't sound like an insult.

Through the onset of re-emerging tiredness, Dalila smiled.

'So, they won – Thoth and Nut. They won enough moonlight to make five new days, and Nut was finally able to give birth to her five children, the next generation of gods. But they have their own stories, and I ought to get at least some sleep.'

Asim made space for his granddaughter on his bed, and she lay beside him without question. He let her sleep, but as she did, he told her a story, of gods and monsters and fear and hope. He couldn't help himself, and it was one she'd never heard before.

'Next time,' he whispered, 'we'll have even greater adventures.'

* * *

Less than an hour later, Dalila was up, and almost late for work. Her grandfather rested by her side, and looked to be in a deep, peaceful sleep. She smiled softly before hurrying out the door, in a rush to get there on time.

It was very close. She'd sprinted the entire way from her house to the minister's and reached with barely a minute to spare. As she donned her apron and brought out the cooking paraphernalia, her heartbeat still reverberating around her body, Dalila thought for a second about stakes and tension. She thought about the story she had shared with her grandfather. It had been so long since they'd connected in a way as meaningful as that – they had both been struggling with the absence of her parents in different ways. But they had been there for each other.

In the midst of all this, Dalila realised she was happy. The story had been a moment that made her happy, and save for her sewing, that was rare for her.

She spent the rest of the night stirring, sprinkling spices, creating something greater than the sum of its parts. This time was a bit different, though. Dalila was paying attention, she was focused. She still found the work tedious and took no pleasure from it, but she was aware of everything that she was doing. Talking to her grandfather had opened her mind in a way it hadn't been for ages. Something about him made her want to appreciate the world around her more, or at least try to.

The early trappings of the sun released her from her responsibilities in the kitchen for the time being. Homeward bound, she took in more on her walk back than she had the countless times she'd walked that same path before.

Once back in her domain, Dalila splashed her face with some water and took a couple of deep breaths. She'd have to leave again soon, as she was painfully aware, but she nonetheless sat by her *jadiy*'s side. He was awake, but tired. He mumbled a few words but Dalila couldn't make them out. She took his hand and squeezed it, and felt her grandfather try to do the same.

She had never seen him this weak before. Dalila felt that terror rise in her again. Her mind seemed deep underwater, and she could scarcely form a thought before she heard him trying to speak again. She could hear the effort in his voice.

'My storyteller. Dalila. I love you. More than I could ever tell you. I love you. Never forget the stories. Keep them alive. Keep them…'

Dalila was in tears. She held on tighter to her grandfather's hand and cried to herself. He lay on the bed, motionless. She did not know how long she sat there. Time seemed too cruel a notion to think about.

Dalila cried most of that day. It would come and go, and it was the same intense grief every time. She didn't go to work. She hoped Sadiki would understand.

The next day, she was hollow. As days came and went, the further away that hollowness seemed, the more intensely it would return. Empty of all feeling, she turned to the one thing that gave her comfort – her sewing. She took out the cloth she had saved and let her fingers do what they wanted. For the first time, she wasn't paying attention, but at least she had something else to do.

Dalila looked at the product once she had finished it, surprising herself. It was a simple shroud, a patchwork of different cloths and materials, but joined together perfectly. In its centre was a small figure that stood out, a multicoloured woman in a sea of dark blue. She was the sky, in all its interminable beauty. The goddess would be there forever – the seamstress would make sure of that.

Nut, Dalila & Fiction (& Me):
A Tangent

I consider plot a necessary intrusion

on what I really want to do,

which is write snappy dialogue.

– Aaron Sorkin

FOR SOME TIME now, I've known that the closest thing in my life to a passion is writing. That is the most I have been able to figure out about myself after nearly two decades of intermittent attempts. Anything beyond that fact, or any attempt to deconstruct or understand it, has never brought much else into the fray.

But, over the past year or two, some of those deconstructions have finally begun to reveal more about me, as well as shedding light on the reasons it took me this long to reach these semi-conclusions. This has something to do with the story, I promise.

First of all – it's taken me this long to try. I have spent the vast majority of my life not writing. I do realise the ridiculousness of that sentence, given that most of my life until now has been my childhood. Still, it's helpful for me to think about the different stages so far, and what I call my intellectual awakening.

That's the pretentious name I use to refer to the part of my life in which the majority of my personality and sense of self were discovered or appeared to cement themselves in me. I realise, too, that this is all due to change before I know it, but I'm sticking to what I know in this moment, because speculating has rarely served me well.

That 'intellectual awakening' of mine occurred sometime while I was at boarding school, which is where I can see an early form of my current relationship to writing developed. I thought myself good at it, better than average, perhaps, but it wasn't something I took seriously at all, nor something I pursued to any non-academic extent. The same is true for a lot of things in my life – without external pressure, I am loath to try anything I don't have to, even if it's something I enjoy.

In the latter stage of my five years at boarding school, there came an emphasis from the higher-ups that the students close to graduating should begin – or even be close to – finding what they want to continue studying or practising once they leave. It is here that a degree of delusion settled in for me. Again, I promise this has something to do with the story.

I really put all my eggs in one basket – film. It seemed reasonable enough; I enjoy watching movies immensely, some friends of mine are studying it too, and every once in a while I come up with a decent script for one. As I entered my final year though, the pretences I had welcomed for so long slowly began to hand me over to reality. It turns out, studying film wasn't something I particularly enjoyed.

I liked spending time with my friends, I liked talking about movies, and any pleasure I derived from the odd script I wrote was completely independent from any of my study. I was bad at film as well (as a subject, at least; filming and editing and various other positions), but what made it worse was that I had no motivation to try, and nothing made me want to improve.

So, I took the only transferrable skill from this soon-to-be-failed endeavour, and thought about it a lot more. I had spent the past several years convincing others and myself that screenwriting was what I wanted to do, what I wanted to pursue, but it became less and less convincing as time wore on. I did, though, see something intrinsic in my enjoyment of writing scripts, something I realised could be found any time I was hitting my stride writing something. That's where I've been for a while since, aware that the purest answer to the question of what I want to do is 'to write', but I have spent neither time nor effort breaking that down, as I mentioned at the start.

To be honest, I spent a long time considering it a cop-out. I come from a family of writers: my father, my aunts and great aunts and uncles, not to mention grandparents, from whom I am at the very least decades removed. It seemed the easy way out, the one people would understand and not have to question, and the one that seems on-brand for me and my background.

For this reason, I think I avoided writing at any length or perceived level of quality because I didn't want to prove myself wrong or right in my characterisation of my writing talent. If I was wrong, I had nothing else to fall back on. If I was right, I'd have to practise and continue doing it, which seemed equally daunting. We're getting closer to how this relates to the story – I'm pretty sure.

* * *

Fast-forward about six months: I had just decided to drop out of university, having realised the course I had chosen was not at all interesting to me. I knew that by leaving I'd be giving myself an endless expanse of free time that I would, in some way or another, have to fill. The only thing I still knew about myself at that point was that I could write, so I thought for a while, then came up with nothing. Around the time the notion of this book started to become a reality, it occurred to me that I hadn't done any decent amount of writing for roughly a year, and that I'd be going in at a serious disadvantage. So, at the suggestion of some people far brighter than me, I started a blog.

Five hundred words a day, that was the target. I did it, which was immensely empowering to see in myself. Not everything I wrote was good, in fact I can confidently say anything of quality in that period of work was the exception and not the rule, but that wasn't at all what was going through my mind at the time. What I saw was a muscle being trained. Every day, hitting that target got easier and easier, and I actually had faith in my own ability to write. It was at this point that I reached a significant conclusion, the first since I had discovered my passion for writing.

That critical realisation was that I much preferred writing non-fiction than fiction. I found it far easier, and I recognised the 'flow' state I sometimes entered while writing popped up almost exclusively during my non-fiction writing. I could write at length for an hour, no sweat. I didn't have to come up with a pretence, or really filter any of my thoughts, but could simply provide a slightly edited real-time description of what was going through my mind. Fiction, though, was a totally different beast.

I don't have the patience to write it. Not yet, at least – I'm working on it. It requires far more effort than its counterpart, which is likely why it took me so long to give it a shot. What I mean by my lack of patience is that I tend to find it frustrating knowing the finer beats of a story, while at the same time having to write each one in detail. My mind goes, *why do I have to write this bit – I know what happens next and how it ends, and this is nowhere near as interesting.* Unfortunately, the voice doesn't go away, either, which means I end up making the whole task more difficult for myself.

Something was different about this story, though. *I told you we'd get here!* I had principally read through the myth and stories of Nut, and had come up with an outline of my own. I know that while I have the capacity to go into great (perhaps too much) detail sometimes, I find it difficult to do so within a pre-existing story or set of ideas.

I was aware, though, that detail was what the story needed if it was to be even remotely interesting in my version, so it occurred to me to create it separately. I honestly cannot describe how excited I felt when I realised this was even an option. So, I opened up a new Word document, and typed the first sentence that came to mind, about a young woman named Dalila.

I knew absolutely nothing about the story I was writing, or the characters, but I just kept adding sentences that, very slowly, started to fill in the gaps. As soon as I recognised an interesting set-up I had accidentally established or wanted to establish, I added it to my rough list of notes that were just as long as the story. I found it far more exciting, I realised: writing without the ending in clear sight.

It must be at least part of the reason I so enjoy writing non-fiction. The blog entries were never planned, never thought about ahead of time, or given any level of preparation at all. I'd start writing, figure out a fun idea, and keep it going as long as I could, until I reached the target. They were messy and, at times, incoherent, but the freedom of the work was something I could not get enough of.

That's what I'm going to try my best to replicate, until that impatience fades away, or no longer presents any issues. I will try until I can match the pace of my writing fiction with non-fiction, until I enjoy it the same amount, until I enjoy both even more than I thought possible, until I'm consistently producing work I'm proud of. I'm not there yet, but I'm more excited than I have been in a while and cannot wait to carve out my niche in the thing I love to do.

On Echo

Life is pain, Highness.

Anyone who tells you differently

is selling something.

– *The Princess Bride*

THE STORY OF Echo in Greek mythology is a short one. I will share it nonetheless, but such was the primary reason I chose not to tell my own version. There was little 'material' to work with from the start, and I struggled to conceive of an original story that did not bear too heavy a resemblance to the classic myth.

In short, I was not sure how to make it my own.

Instead of casting aside the notion of writing about the character entirely, though, I thought it might be interesting to discuss it in more detail, drawing on parts of my life and shared or universal themes that exist in the story. But first, the actual story:

Zeus, who was perennially occupied by consorting with mortal women behind his wife's back, also happened to be king of the gods. This ended up being bad news for the Oread (mountain nymph), Echo. Zeus charged her, without her consent or choice, as was his style, with distracting his wife, Hera. The goddess was constantly teeming with jealousy, trying to catch her husband in the act and punish all those involved.

Echo would comply by engaging the queen of the gods in long-winded, distracting conversations, talking endlessly, filling the time while Zeus cavorted. Hera eventually caught on to the nymph's tactic, and in her typically vengeful ways, she cursed Echo for her loquaciousness with only being able to repeat the last words another person had just said.

In the second part of her story, Echo encountered a beautiful man, to whom she was unable to speak. Narcissus was gorgeous, and he knew it. One day, lost in a forest and separated from his friends, he called out 'Is anyone there?' Echo, given the opportunity, repeated his words. He shouted again 'Let's come together', to which Echo rushed to him and repeated his words. However, Narcissus spurned Echo, and she was left alone, despairing. Later on, Narcissus came across a lake, and fell in love with his own reflection. Unable to move, he slowly died in that spot. Echo mourned and grieved for him before she, too, died. She left behind only her voice.

Echo is one of my absolute favourite figures in the Greek myths, which is somewhat uncharacteristic of me, given my usual aversion to tragic endings. The reasons I have been able to deduce about why this story in particular appeals to me are varied. Firstly, it's a beautiful example of what a lot of mythologies from around the world sought to do. Besides fuelling a religious public, it offered a satisfying and supernatural explanation to a simple, natural phenomenon – an echo.

No one at the time could have accurately offered a better justification behind an echo, and so this story was what remained. As someone fascinated with myths and stories in general, I love the notion that a storyteller came up with this idea, and through its staying power and lack of appreciable competition, the story of Echo remained.

Above this, though, I think my primary draw to the

story is the simple theme of communication as it pertains to Echo particularly. At the start of her myth, Echo is drafted by Zeus to deceive his wife with only words – what else would a mountain nymph have in her arsenal against a goddess? Importantly, though, she uses talking and gossip and distracting conversation, each clear examples of her communicative strengths, to fulfil her role as an agent of interference between Zeus and Hera.

The queen of the gods' retribution, I think, can be attributed to fear as much as anger. Of course, her actions were obviously steeped in revenge, but to me it suggests an equal discomfort at the knowledge that she could have been thwarted for so long with just words. Echo's curse, to only be able to repeat what has most recently been said, would protect Hera or any other goddess from falling victim to the same trick again.

The story of Echo and Narcissus is, in a way, a continuation of the same theme. Narcissus, too, is 'deceived' by words – in this case, his own. He falls in love with the sound of his own voice, and in doing so, dooms himself. Different versions of the story include as an explanation of his condition, a curse placed upon him by the goddess of revenge Nike, who took pity on Echo after he scorned her.

Echo, in a way, is the physical embodiment of his downfall. It is her voice that he hears and falls in love with, and it is her voice that he ultimately rejects. And so, I would argue, the story of Echo is the story of unrequited love (for Narcissus, too), of unspoken words, but chiefly one of communication gone awry.

This theme of communication resonates deeply with me. For most of my life, though it didn't really come into focus until my time at boarding school, I have generally found it difficult to express myself due to my social anxiety. In the original myth and the various retellings of it I have encountered, the parts of the story that I connect with most are whenever Echo attempts to communicate, knowing full well what she is trying to say, but ultimately fails. It is a sentiment and failure I know well, and for me, it only adds to the desperation and hopelessness this character has come to represent.

Hopelessness, paired with a sense of injustice, is yet another key aspect of the story, I find. Through no fault of her own, Echo is forcibly enlisted to help Zeus, thus enabling the curse his wife would inflict upon her. The hopelessness and helplessness are only further intensified once Echo meets Narcissus. She is unable to fight the dichotomy of loving him, and knowing that he loves only himself, all the while incapable of expressing her own thoughts.

To continue unpacking the theme of communication (no, I'm still not done with that), I think it is more universally relevant than it may appear. To invoke a cliché, humans are social creatures, and the importance of communication is evident in every aspect of our lives. The ability to connect with others is what defines us, and yet it is also something that we so often take for granted.

Narcissus chooses to forego this, falling in love with himself to the detriment of his connection with everything and everyone around him. In Echo's case, the choice is made for her, and we must watch as the two characters slowly waste away in those lonely circumstances.

I find it particularly important, then, that while Narcissus fades into nothingness, Echo does too, but leaves something crucial behind – her voice. The thing that tormented her in life outliving her, and leaving a reminder of the tragic life to which it owes its origin. The story of Echo is a reminder of what can happen when communication fails, and I think it is a story that everyone can learn from.

Like other myths in its canon, it features divine intervention and supernatural forces, but unlike most of its contemporaries, I think there is a moral and human truth in Echo's story that makes it as personally affecting as it did at the time of its conception.

Luke

And in my wisdom I can see,

Go not with so much haste from me,

My brilliance, my shining sea,

So daintily away it goes.

WALKING TO THE station, Luke was almost disappointed he wouldn't feel the same brisk air on the train. Carriage 4, seat 26. He checked his ticket again – yep. He exhaled and plunged his hand and the ticket back into his left coat pocket, leaving only his face exposed to the elements, the drizzling spray of rain stinging him, but he didn't mind. Luke was refreshed and ready, and the cold world around him only caffeinated him even more.

It was a fifteen-minute walk from the house. Josie had offered to drive him, but it was almost noon when he left and she was still in her pyjamas – he could tell it was an offer she was hoping he would refuse. Luke took the hint and left a few minutes later, happy to be outside for a while.

He smiled to himself. That thought must have belonged to someone else, because Luke was not a person anyone would guess spent time outside. He was a poet – a job one could do from literally anywhere – yet he rarely left his one-bedroom flat. He went to work, sure, but he had been assured by his family and his one friend that the coffee shop he worked at two tube stops away didn't qualify as 'going outside'.

Luke crossed the road, and an old lady in a car a hundred yards away from him honked with unexpected gusto. She was driving one of those tiny cars from the early aughts that everyone seemed to have in the countryside. He was glad Josie had at least gone with something different, from this decade. Not that she ever needed to use it.

He turned the corner onto the main road, off Josie's side street. The old lady turned too, maintaining her impressively slow speed as she squinted her sharp eyes at Luke before passing him.

Luke was glad he had chosen to walk. He would have done so even if Josie's offer to drive him had been sincere. He thought of it as a short interim. He had passed an 'interesting' weekend at his sister's house, and on that chilly Monday morning, the walk felt like a chance to cool off mentally. The train ride would be a psychologically busy one, Luke knew. He was a chronic overthinker and was enjoying this fresh air and the chance to dull his mind a bit before the full force of his mental faculties hit him on the train.

* * *

In his seat, Luke put on his noise-cancelling headphones and hugged his backpack protectively. The carriage was virtually empty, but his mind was loud enough on its own. The backpack was an ersatz teddy bear; Luke released his tension into his arms and tightened his grip on the suffocating bag.

It wasn't long before scenes from last night flashed out of his short-term memory and into the private screening room at the front of his mind.

Dinner. Josie had made a mushroom risotto. It was her go-to recipe to impress and Luke was not complaining. As a starter, there was a simple Greek salad topped with olives and feta that he felt obligated to sample at least. He hated salads and she knew it. Her husband ate nothing; he had a bowl of salad in front of him that he'd lean down to smell every once in a while. He didn't need to eat, but said the aroma reminded him of home.

Josie and Zeus had been married for four months, now – together for three years. Yes, he was the god, and yes, it was weird to think about. When Hera left him after millennia of infidelity, Zeus grew lonely and bored. To solve the latter issue, he came to earth, traded his godly visage for a chiselled jaw, stormy grey eyes, and short greying beard. Quite the fall from grace, Luke had thought at first. He'd tried to enquire a little more but any mention of Hera sent Zeus into a sulk. Answers seemed to be in short supply.

Anyway, then he met Josie. The two were just good together. Simply perfect – as long as one didn't think too much about the god stuff. Josie quit her job, and the pair lived in a homey two-storey cottage in Devon.

Luke helped himself to a second serving of the risotto, almost missing a glance between Josie and Zeus. Before he could enjoy another bite of the food, Josie piped up.

'Luke, it's been so nice having you here this weekend. Right, Zeus?'

'Yes, definitely,' Zeus chimed in – it sounded rehearsed. Josie continued, a bit nervously.

'But we actually asked you over for a reason, Luke. Nothing serious – in fact, it's great news.'

Luke set down his fork and looked at his sister. He saw a gentle pleading in her eyes. To his right, Zeus sniffed his salad again and smiled. Josie ignored him.

'I – we – are a bit worried about you,' she said.

Luke didn't like where this was going. No matter how many times he told her or their parents, they never grasped that he was content. They always thought they knew better, and that they were helping by interfering. Luke kept a neutral expression as Josie continued.

'I know you haven't done any new poetry in ages. I know that you hate working at the coffee shop, and now I hear it's where you're spending most of your time. Twenty-five seems plenty old to graduate from that kind of job into something… better.'

About to rattle off his usual conciliatory reassurances, Luke paused. That last bit stood out to him.

'Wait, who's been telling you this stuff?' His voice was angrier than he'd meant it to be. He didn't expect his expression was any kinder.

'Well, between Zeus keeping an eye on you and what Sophie told me last week, it sounded like you were in a bit of a bad place.'

At this, Zeus suddenly remembered that he was a part of the conversation. He looked at Josie, his expression unreadable.

Luke was still reeling from what he'd just heard. The almighty Zeus, king of the gods, his immortal brother-in-law, had been spying on him. What really threw him, though, was that Sophie had been talking to his sister. Luke felt a knot tangling up his insides.

'You spoke to Sophie?'

'Yeah.'

Luke turned to Zeus. 'And you've been trailing me? For how long?'

'A couple weeks or so. I am not sure; time passes so slowly here. But Josie and I thought it the best way to make sure you were alright.'

'What, so I miss a few phone calls and suddenly you're spying on me and – and calling my ex-girlfriend?'

Josie leaned forward. 'She reached out to me. Said you weren't being yourself, and you never got back to her about Puffle.'

'What's a Puffle?' Zeus said, the conversation just becoming interesting for him.

'That's not the point. I just wanted to check in on you.' Josie looked at her brother. Luke returned her gaze. He looked down and exhaled.

'Wow. Okay. Let me recap – let me know if I've missed anything. My little sister and her godly husband have been keeping tabs on me for weeks. Plus, you've been talking to my ex about how badly I'm apparently doing and about how she wants my cat.'

'Oh, the cat. I'm fairly sure that cat hates you, Luke. Sorry, but it's true,' Zeus interjected. He didn't look that sorry.

'And for what? You invited me out here to the middle of nowhere to do what? Pity me?'

Josie remained calm. She can't have been expecting a quiet response from Luke, and given what they had just told him, his reaction almost seemed justified.

'We invited you here,' she said, her tone even and empathetic, 'because we want to help.'

'Help how?' Luke replied, the tension in his chest pulsing, slower now.

'Well, I know with how much work you've taken on at the coffee shop, you've barely given yourself a day off. No time to write, to do anything.'

'Yeah, so? I need the money. Poetry doesn't exactly pay the bills.'

'We know that, and that's why Zeus and I want to help out. Take some of the pressure off.'

'Yes, it's really nothing,' Zeus said. He waved his hands over his empty glass, and it filled to the brim with glimmering gold coins. 'You could take a break, go on holiday, maybe. Your parents bought a car and are planning a trip to – where was it – Hawaii? No, Tahiti. Anyway, you could do the same.'

'You could just relax for a bit, Luke. Spend some time writing. Do whatever you want to.'

Emotions flooded into his mind – good, mostly bad, and begging for a chance at centre stage. Anger prevailed.

'I don't want your pity; I don't want your handouts or money. Good night.'

Luke's voice was just loud enough to be heard, but he upped the volume as he headed to the guest bedroom. He called out, 'Thanks for dinner, Josie. The salad was delicious.'

An echo trailed him back to the dinner table.

* * *

Back on the train, Luke re-evaluated his decision. He agreed with himself. He didn't need the money – he didn't want it.

148

Still, though, he hoped that the events of last night had stirred up enough in his mind to write something – he hadn't done anything in weeks. That's why he took more hours at the coffee shop, because he didn't know what else to do in the interim. By the time he'd come home from work, he was always too tired to think, much less write. It had become a vicious cycle.

Luke loosened the death grip on his bag and took out his notebook and pen, in the unlikely case genius struck him then and there. Besides noting down the events of last night, all he managed was a bored haiku:

My sister, god-wife,
Pities me and loves salads.
The god just sniffs them.

* * *

Luke was still angry – the walk had only done so much to cleanse him – but there was a little jealousy mixed in this time. His brain hadn't been working fast enough to involve it last night, but it was here now – and Luke hated it. He hated what the jealousy said about him. He knew Josie had sensed it that morning. But why should she get the money and the domestic bliss? He's done the hard work, all his life and relentlessly, and he wasn't going to take a shortcut. He wasn't going to let it be for nothing.

* * *

The train arrived in London a short time later. Luke went through the motions, in and out of the public transport system. The sounds of trains and people that normally pervaded the air seemed dull, like a lead shield blocked the outside world from disturbing him. He thought about writing and about work. He thought about Josie and about how she was right, in a way.

He knew, when he decided he wanted to do poetry, that he'd have to get a job to provide some (any) income, and he hadn't even succeeded at getting the measly job he wanted. No, he didn't work at a bookshop like he had imagined he would, he worked at a fancy coffee shop, serving coffee concoctions to like-minded creatives – who actually had some money in the bank. He could make good coffee, though, and it was a small internal victory for him when he saw Josie still using filter coffee that he knew tasted like mud.

Luke didn't register that he was back home until he found himself fiddling with the key in his lock. He heard a disturbed mew as he opened the door, and saw Puffle staring at him at the end of the corridor. She mewed once more and walked away through a doorway on the left, uninterested.

She doesn't hate me, Luke thought. He didn't know if he cared.

Luke's apartment was small and devoid of any interesting characteristics. Even still, he knew he'd have to find somewhere cheaper to live soon – he wasn't splitting rent with Sophie any more.

Down a corridor from his front door were three doors. His bedroom, on the right, was scarcely bigger than his bed, and there were still scuff marks on the wall from when Luke had tried to fit a small nightstand in. His bathroom was equally featureless, save for the cat that spent its sleeping and waking hours lying underneath the heated towel rack. Luke's study was as small as the rest of the flat suggested, with a crowded bookcase, a hideous blue sofa, and a desk crammed in.

Luke showered and unpacked, and before long it was as if he'd never left. Except for that feeling, that uneasy tug in his gut that had followed him out from the West Country. It was there as he put his notebook in the drawer, and it was there as he logged in on his phone to book a shift for early the next morning.

The study was Luke's favourite room. At this time of day, yellow light seeped in through the window, lighting the particulates in the air like a shower of gold dust. He sank into his desk chair. Luke didn't know what to do with the rest of his day – he could go for a walk or catch a movie, but nothing really appealed to him. He hadn't spoken to his university friends in a few months now, and didn't feel like breaking that streak any time soon.

Luke knew what he should do. His eyes drifted to the desk drawer in which he had stashed his notebook. In recent weeks, it had barely seen the light of day; having it sit on his desk was a daily reminder for Luke of his ineptitude and lack of focus, so into the drawer it went.

Turning instead to his collection of books, he picked one at random. He'd read all of them before but had the strange quality of forgetting mostly everything about them when he finished. It was a quality that served him well when he was editing his own work. Or so he liked to remember.

The book Luke picked was *Normal People*, by Sally Rooney. He felt as though any time he read a book, no matter its quality, he found something to learn. Each time he sifted through the pages of this one, Luke felt the need to focus on his relationships, on the people in his life. Last time he had read it was just last month, a week or two before Sophie had broken up with him. Not a stellar review for this moment. He read the beginning, sunk his mind into the world of the book for a minute, and put it away.

Without thinking, Luke took out his notebook and scribbled down an idea. It was the tail end of a thought he'd found interesting, and when he stopped writing to read it over, he didn't even understand it. Worse, he didn't understand why he had chosen to write it down. He flipped through the notebook; dozens of these meaningless fragments of inspiration filled the yellowing pages, each teetering on a see-saw of tangibility and intangibility. It was like when you remind yourself to do something, reinforce that thought, and still forget to do it. And it just kept going.

That was another reason he couldn't take their money, Luke thought as he read his ramblings. What would he even do with infinite resources? He was fairly certain ideas weren't included. His issues were exacerbated, not caused, by his day job.

Once Luke had reached these unpleasant conclusions and put his notebook back in the drawer, the crimson sky of the setting sun had shifted into a wine-dark purple. Luke was considering this imagery when his phone pinged with a message telling him that his shift started in twelve hours. After a long weekend and insomnia last night post-train wreck at dinner, he decided a night of sleep in his own bed would probably do him some good. He put out some food for an ungrateful Puffle and slumped onto his bed.

Ever since Luke had met Zeus for the first time, and had his entire understanding of the natural world turned on its head, he didn't trust his dreams anymore. Well, no more than the little amount of trust he thought one ought to place in their dreams. He could just about wrap his head around the supernatural in his daily life because he just never saw it. He didn't visit Josie and Zeus often and had heard little to no mention of the rest of the gods. His dreams, though, were a completely different territory.

They were weird, but the problem was that they just kept getting weirder. There were monsters and heroes and mysterious forces doing their bidding from the unseen lands. It was as though a veil had been lifted and Luke had been granted access to the special wavelength of dreams. He eventually got used to their perfect clarity, only for the strangest element to then be introduced a few weeks ago.

'Is this thing on?' he heard tonight. Zeus always started this way. 'I jest, of course. We're glad you got home safely. How is Puffle? Never mind. I only have a brief message this evening, from Josie. She wants you to know that there are no ill feelings about last night, and we would love to have you back soon. Josie also asks that you reconsider our offer – just give it some more thought. Anyway, that's all from me. When is your next shift? Ah, six-thirty a.m. – an early riser must you be!'

Luke woke with a start. A few seconds later, his alarm went off. Olympian wake-up calls were very punctual, it would seem. Zeus had been talking to Luke in his dreams a couple of days a week. The content of his dreaming interludes varied, ranging from messages from Josie and iffy stock tips to a dramatic reading of Britney Spears' 'Toxic'. He always woke up rested after the soliloquies, though, so he suffered through them.

Walking to work, Luke appreciated the quietness of a London on the verge of waking up. It was like the tide rolling back before a massive wave, one the city endured every day.

As a part of other people's early morning routine, Luke started his day even earlier. At work, he silently prepped all the machines for another session of abuse, cleaning up places last night's shift had missed, and just plain waiting. The first few customers were always his favourites – they were just as miserable as he was. There were few people up at that time that didn't have to be.

As the morning dragged on, the comfort of routine masking the passage of time to Luke, the unbearables shuffled in. The twenty-somethings with lofty ideals, always-new laptops, and complicated coffee orders. Free Wi-Fi and caffeine were all the inspiration they needed in a day. He loathed them. They were everything he didn't want to be – and exactly how he dreaded he would be if he took up Josie and Zeus on their offer. At least with the coffee shop Luke knew he wasn't wasting his time entirely; he couldn't say the same about everything else.

Luke also knew that Zeus was a big part in the choice

he had made. Like the carefree coffee-drinkers, Zeus represented something Luke hated: power that doesn't care about or respect its own power. For the god, this small act was something intensely impactful that took little more effort than blinking.

Luke spent the next week second-guessing himself, ignoring calls from Josie, and trying to ignore Zeus' dream monologues. One day, though, something happened he definitely hadn't expected. Josie walked into the coffee shop. Despite all of the overthinking throughout the past week and the way they left things off, Luke was relieved to see his sister. He quickly made her favourite drink, black coffee – unsweetened and with no milk, like an animal. He clocked out and joined her at a table outside.

'How did you get here?' he finally asked. He used to joke that Devon felt like a suburb of a suburb of a suburb of London but still, it was far.

Josie looked behind Luke and he turned to see an eagle casually sitting on a bench down the road, eyeing passers-by. Luke laughed.

'I felt like I needed to apologise in person – that was a lot to spring on you last weekend and I should have been a little more delicate. I also probably should have mentioned that I talked to Sophie. How is Puffle, by the way?'

'Oh, she hates me, but we're working on it. And there's no reason to apologise, Josie – I probably could have handled it better.'

Josie smiled. 'Not to bring up a sore subject – and this is the last time I'll ask, I promise – have you given any more thought to our offer?'

'Definitely. Too much, actually.'

'And?'

'I'm in.'

The words seemed strange in Luke's mouth, but his subconscious was glad to fill him in. The change of his decision only really took one consideration: his sister's perspective. Once the fog of myopia had lifted, Luke saw what was hidden behind it, just a sister with the means to help, and desperate willingness to.

Luke would be doing her a favour as much as they would be for him. She just wanted to involve herself in her brother's life. When he had rebuffed their first offer at dinner, she wasn't angry – she was hurt. Accepting their offer would be his chance to actually do something with a power that went almost entirely underappreciated, he reasoned.

Josie grinned and then cleared her throat. In an instant, Zeus was sitting in the seat beside Josie and the eagle behind Luke had disappeared.

'You made the right choice, Luke,' he said.

'You really did,' said Josie. 'Just wait till you hear what Zeus has lined up for you.'

'What?' Luke said, his interest suddenly piqued.

Zeus smiled. 'Let's just say your work has been commissioned by some pretty important people. Gods are extremely vain, after all.'

'You're kidding!'

'Not at all. But don't tell them I said that.'

Josie chuckled. 'Oh, this is going to be a lot of fun.'

A Big Hero in a Bigger World

Historians are accustomed to condone

the faults of a great man by arguing that

they were the faults of his time.

But a man shows his greatness by the measure

in which he surpasses the standards of his age.

– Laurence Binyon, *Akbar*

GILGAMESH WOULD NOT live forever. He was certain of that now. *It was never your place.* The voice of divinity rang in his ears. Ishtar was still bitter, it would seem. *Your final days have already been written.*

He did not need the immortal's reminder. She had no power over his mind in this moment. She revealed nothing that hadn't echoed in his own thoughts for the past six days.

'I know, Ishtar,' Gilgamesh said, 'I know I'm going to die.'

If she had heard the hero-king, the goddess gave no indication. Nor did the man across from him. The immortal ferryman just continued to row – Urshanabi rarely spoke.

The pair sat in silence, as they had done for almost a week now. The sea made no noise. Gilgamesh might have once thought this unnatural – they had seen empty skies and nary a wave since departing – but he now knew there was nothing natural about the gods and their ways. Did they take pity on him after his plight? Was there something more foul awaiting him in his home of Uruk that they were eagerly nudging him towards? He did not know. And he was tired of answers.

The boat churned forward. It was simple – long and narrow, with an enchanted rudder beneath the stern, steering towards wherever the ferryman was going. Gilgamesh sat on a thick plank that went across the boat, Urshanabi in an identical seat opposite. The sparse remains of provisions lay at their feet, but Gilgamesh was in no mood to eat. The endless travel that defined his quest, his encounter with the Scorpion People and the undying mortal – he was, by this point, world-weary and morose. Urshanabi just rowed.

Neither had slept in days. Gilgamesh had too much on his mind, but he wondered if his companion was even capable of it. The ferryman had shown no signs of fatigue, of slowing down. He kept the same pace, wielding the oars precisely as they propelled the vessel into the horizon.

Against his apparent better judgement, Gilgamesh's mind went to Enkidu. Created by the gods to humble the tyrannical leader Gilgamesh could scarcely remember being, the pair found in each other a worthy opponent and kindred spirit.

Their friendship had been brief but beautifully intense, the kind that made those few months together feel like no time had passed, an eternity unto itself. The understanding one finds themselves capable of for the first time, only to have it ripped from their clutches. They made each other better and stronger, but progress isn't permanent. Gilgamesh felt that now, especially. When Enkidu was killed, the person Gilgamesh had started to be perished with him. He held back a curse at Ishtar for the theft of Enkidu's life.

'Tell me about him.'

The hero was startled out of his train of thought. Urshanabi looked at him, his expression as impossible to read as always. Gilgamesh had wondered if it hid multitudes or a hollowness. He returned to the surprise of the question.

'What?'

'Your friend, the wild man. Tell me about him.'

Gilgamesh was bemused by the sudden interest.

Nevertheless, the prompt gave him the chance to put into words what had been clouding his mind for days.

'Enkidu was... unpredictable,' he told the ferryman. 'As a child, I was taught the ways of order over chaos, of power over randomness. Such was to be expected in a leader of Uruk – or so my father had thought. Enkidu was my polar opposite.'

Urshanabi gave a nod, an invitation to continue. But Gilgamesh did not know where in their story to start. Its end was what preoccupied him. He could recount their epic battle against each other, which Gilgamesh had won, but only just. He could tell the ferryman what he saw in Enkidu's eyes when they had fought – not an ounce of hatred, just skill and a desire to stay alive. Enkidu, created by the gods to foil his pride, carried no ill will towards him.

Gilgamesh could speak of the unspeakable agony he felt – the righteous indignation at the gods for killing his friend, boring a hole at the same time into his own faith. He could say all this and more, but it wouldn't feel right.

'One ought not speak ill of the gods,' the hero said finally, 'their memories have outlived empires before us. It would be unwise to test their patience.'

Gilgamesh could feel Urshanabi's eyes on him, looking for the meaning behind his platitude. The ferryman relaxed his face and focused once again on rowing, his silent assessment apparently complete.

'A story for another time, then,' he said flatly. Gilgamesh could detect no judgement in his voice.

The truth was as simple as he had laid out – he was a man of few facades. Gilgamesh did not trust himself to recount the story of Enkidu without bringing upon himself the same fate. He would not be able to hide the bitterness, the rage and the grief that even still stewed in his brain. The conspirators of his failed quest for immortality.

'What do you know of Utnapishtim?' he found himself asking the ferryman after a while.

'Ah, the mortal amongst gods, purveyor of eternal youth. Nothing but a misunderstood loner, if you ask me.'

Gilgamesh looked to the heavens, awaiting some force of nature, some punishment. But nothing came. Either the gods cared little about their conversation, or it was a token of their disdain for Utnapishtim. Urshanabi followed his gaze and smiled.

'Fear not, Gilgamesh. They know I'm right.'

Some tension left the hero's body. He did not know why he trusted Urshanabi so implicitly, but he did not question it. Answers seemed already within reach.

'What do you mean, misunderstood?' he said.

'Utnapishtim is a young god, as I'm sure you know. Born a mortal, he was chosen to build a ship and preserve the natural world from a flood. It was all luck, though. That's all this game of immortality is. He wasn't chosen for any particular reason. Like any of us, he could have been born an insect, or a god, or never have been born at all. This whole game is chance. And yet he stands there, at the mouths of rivers, doing with his eternities as the other immortals do – nothing.'

Gilgamesh thought back to his trials – the six sleepless nights, the magic plant he failed to protect. Utnapishtim had been reluctant to help him, had told him to give up his search.

What had originally appeared selfish, though, now seemed more like quiet disillusion. The young god knew the reality of what the hero sought, and he knew, too, that achieving it was not a matter of one's choice or will. First, Gilgamesh failed to remain awake for six days and nights. Then, he retrieved the rare flower of youth – only for a serpent to steal it from him.

What he had been attributing to a moral or physical failure made far more sense once accepted as chance. Our responsibilities only account for so much. The trick of it all, Gilgamesh realised, was that we still had to try. Luck is many things, but not passive. One must act in order to be a part of the gamble. The dice do not throw themselves.

He caught a smile of recognition from Urshanabi. The ferryman saw the hero's mind at work. It was the calm pride of a teacher who knew they were being understood.

'Can I ask you a question, Gilgamesh?'

'Yes. Yes, of course.'

'Why was it immortality you sought?'

Gilgamesh took a deep breath. It was an answer he had considered for ages.

'When Enkidu died, it affected me deeply. I understood the price of love, the undeniable pain that comes as part of the deal. But not having love in one's life seemed like the wrong lesson to learn. I thought, then, that perhaps there was a way around that suffering and hurt. For others, at least. No one I love would have to watch me die, as I did watch Enkidu. More than that, though, with immortality I would finally be able to do good forever, be a good king to my people, and be a positive constant that could be relied upon when needed.'

'Very noble, indeed. But your goodness was never what I was questioning.' Urshanabi paused and smiled. 'Be *selfish*, Your Majesty.'

Gilgamesh did not like this prompt. Further still, he disliked that he knew exactly what his reply was. It had been echoing in his mind for weeks, as he'd crossed oceans and mountains in search of immortality. He was selfish. He knew that already. Enkidu's death had been extremely painful for him, but he was ashamed. Ashamed that the one thought that remained with him was a life without meaning. Insignificance.

'I don't want to be forgotten,' he said in a quiet voice. Guilt, and a strange sense of relief rushed through him.

'I see,' said the ferryman. 'Well, I can quite confidently say there's little danger of that happening. Your lived experiences may seem small now, especially given the ending you did not expect, but the story of your life is one rife with greatness. Besides, immortality isn't as good as it may seem. Imagine the boredom and apathy required to kill a man like Enkidu, for nothing but a scorned proposal and a slaughtered bovine.'

Gilgamesh smiled, his first in some time. There was a twinge of sadness, too, but he could feel it receding into a corner of his mind. All that seemed so long ago already, events he imagined might seem fanciful at another time or place.

'You are a great man, Gilgamesh. And a great king. Much lies in store for you yet, but I can confidently say your legacy is secure enough.' Just as he finished speaking, Urshanabi slowed down the stroke of the oars. Gilgamesh choked back a sob when he saw why.

He was home. Uruk. He felt comforted by the sights of places he knew well, places a past version of him had thought of as his entire world. He was different, and it would be wrong to assume his home hadn't changed, too.

'You have an eternity of memory ahead of you. But be wise, Your Majesty. Don't take anything you have in your life for granted.'

Gilgamesh realised what his companion was saying, and who he was. The immortal ferryman of the dead, Urshanabi had seen all that is capable of corrupting a soul. He was speaking from experience.

The boat pulled into the harbour. Sailors eyed it warily, backing away from the vessel, out of some primal instinct, perhaps. Gilgamesh disembarked and looked at Urshanabi once more. He wanted to say something, to convey his gratitude, but nothing came to mind.

Urshanabi looked at him, understanding.

'Be well, Gilgamesh, and thank you for your company. It will be some time before we see each other again. Until then, do not think of me.'

He got the message and stood there watching as the boat left the harbour and shimmered into black just before the horizon.

The next few days went by extremely slowly. Royal duties to oversee, people to meet, and an endless list of chores that Gilgamesh found himself enjoying more than he ever had.

He would ask his citizens what they had been doing, take an interest in the stories they told him. In exchange, he told his own. Tales from his time away. In this trade of memories,

Gilgamesh finally understood what Urshanabi had told him. Real immortality is not a sole endeavour, it is built by the people around you.

On Meaninglessness

I do not want people to be very agreeable,

as it saves me the trouble of liking them

a great deal.

– Jane Austen

THE STORY OF Gilgamesh is not one I knew before researching it for a story. It being a myth – one of the first – I was expecting a long slog of material to read through, a collection of disparate, tangentially related tales. I have a fondness for those stories; some of my favourite gods and heroes (Loki, Anubis, Calypso) have existed in many different forms and situations, crafted and drafted by different poets and writers. Moreover, they have gone on to have their canons extended and added to by storytellers through the ages, especially in the past century or so of writing.

Gilgamesh is different in that regard, though. He was, by all accounts, a real man. A real king of the land of Uruk. His story tells of partially divine parentage, sure, his mother supposedly the goddess Ninsun and his father a priest-king. So, liberties were taken, details embellished, until a relative divide presented itself. A divide between Gilgamesh the man, and Gilgamesh the demigod hero. At the time of their highest popularity, no such divide was considered, and he was revered as a supernatural force among men. Now, of course, it is easy enough to distinguish between the two.

That is what interested me most when I began researching the character/man. I am an avid reader of myths, and while I have sampled stories from a variety of cultures, and chosen the versions I wanted to tell, I have inevitably missed more than I have read. That notwithstanding, the correlation between a real person and myth is something I had yet to discover before reading of Gilgamesh. And the fact that it stands as the oldest piece of mythic literature leads me to think more about the significance of the partial reality of it all.

Myths are products of public consciousness or, at the very least, sustained because of it. The people of Gilgamesh's time and place had a pantheon of gods – as did more familiar cultures like the Greeks, Egyptians – in addition to heroes and mortals to populate the stories. But these same people saw in one of their leaders, King Gilgamesh of Uruk, a lasting quality. They proved that the supernatural element is but one of many factors that can make a story last. That brings me to the overarching themes of the epic – legacy and immortality – and where we diverge for a short while from reality.

Even before setting off on his quest for eternal youth, spurred on by the death of his close friend, Gilgamesh had already a number of feats under his belt. He had rescued the goddess Ishtar (their relationship would subsequently sour, as I refer to in the story), and vanquished a forest demon, and defeated the wild man Enkidu in battle before befriending him.

Long before he lay at his friend's side, overcome with grief and a recognition of his own mortality, he was an accomplished hero. But, of course, none of these exploits were what he focused on. In fact, he condemned them and questioned their significance in a life that he now realised was doomed to ultimate extinction. In today's parlance, Gilgamesh had an existential crisis.

Now, by no means do I suffer from any serious mental conditions, but I sympathise with those who do. The extent of my struggles has been a crippling social anxiety, and delusions of my own intelligence, but those are eminently solvable issues. But, and I would resent any references to my young age in relation to this fact, I have undergone an occasional instance in my life that I would describe as an existential crisis of sorts. None in a while, thankfully, but I've come to think about them in detail.

Some have been related to my social insecurities, in and out of school, and some I can fairly easily trace back to conclusions reached about the world in my philosophy class. My point is that, like Gilgamesh, I have found myself questioning the meaning of the things in my life, and to a degree, my existence as a whole.

I have also been extremely fortunate in life – not demigod-king-of-Uruk fortunate, but a lot of things have gone right for me. *Shah* may mean 'king', but it brings little more than meaning to the table. Regardless of one's position, though, I think it can be very easy to become suddenly disillusioned with the world around us, a world we tend to take for granted.

The second that a fact we have lived with all our lives is challenged, and crumbles, it can leave you doubting the foundations of your core beliefs. With me, that's been a combination of some cruel metaphysical conclusions about reality, and doubts about my place in inescapable parts of life. With Gilgamesh, it was the sudden and torturous loss of his friend.

When confronted with a severe lack of answers and certainty, I found myself desperate to change that in any way I could. I compulsively search for certainty, routine and answers wherever I can in my life. This manifested in Gilgamesh as a desire for immortality. It was a guarantee that he would never inflict the same sense of meaninglessness and dread in himself or others, as his actions would live on as he did. It was crucial, though, that this fantastical goal was one he wouldn't reach.

I have experienced, in my own quest for reliability and routine, that what we search for is often much harder to find than we believe or are ready to admit, and not nearly as effective as the ideal we hold in our mind. At the time of writing, I have moved around a lot just this past year and have felt the dwindling effects of consistency and certainty as I still pined after them.

For Gilgamesh, immortality was not the answer. It was a solution, yes, but not to the problem from which he suffered. He would condemn himself to a never-ending life, with no surprise nor any of the things he took pleasure in during his mortal reign. More importantly, though, through his failure to attain the 'gift' of eternity, he was afforded a legacy greater than an immortal's. That, I think, is a fine fate for – quite literally – the man, the myth, the legend.

As for me – I'm content enough with my mortality. For now, at least.

Calypso & Time

The torrent's free at last, my brain

Can burst forth with all which has simmered

In trenches deep and dark inside,

Not always, though, and still eyes glimmered,

The sun, the sand, the smoking rind.

WHAT IS PARADISE?

It is a question she once thought of often, but not anymore. Paradise meant nothing. Good meant nothing.

Time meaning little more to her, either, Calypso remained in her bed, in no rush to start her day. Even if she missed it, another one would always come.

She stared at the ceiling of her cave. Crystals shimmered purple and blue, catching a light that always seemed to be there, perfectly placed. Perfect meant nothing to her, either.

She rose slowly from her bed. Morning crept in from outside and carried to the island's mistress the scent of flowers and sea breeze. Calypso always tried not to notice. She thought it a small act of defiance, a rejection of her gilded prison, but no. Even apathy was a luxury that only extended so far.

She dressed for the day as she always did, in the same simple blue dress she had worn for countless days before. It was something she used to bemoan, one more thing that contributed to her anger, but that had faded in time. She no longer felt as strongly as she used to. She did not believe herself capable of it. What was there in her home, the idyllic island Ogygia, that could inspire indefinite feeling? There was no such thing, no magic she could even fathom, that could usurp the inevitability of time.

For time was Calypso's jailer as much as the gods. Those new immortals had filled her with an acrimony and a rage she'd once thought intense enough to span the ages; time had emptied her, left her numb.

* * *

Stepping outside, Calypso smiled. It was faint and vacant, reflecting muscle memory more than any feelings at all.

It had once been a genuine smile. Her island's beauty was undeniable and divine. Hills of forest and meadows lay but a few paces from her cave, in front of where she now stood on the beach. At the heart of the island lay a lake that had once been a source of comfort and tranquillity for the goddess.

She did not look over her shoulder. Behind her, the horizon loomed. Interminable and infinite in its cruelty, it had once offered the goddess hope. She had spent years, decades sitting on the sand, her eyes never leaving the line. The division between the realms of Zeus and Poseidon bore no figures, no shapes ever disturbed the blue. The image her soft green eyes took in was unchanging. The vindictive anger of the cerulean sea and sky had been absorbed into the young Calypso, now faded.

She passed the afternoon like a phantom. Calypso did as she always did. Novelty hadn't been present, hadn't been a comfort, for millennia.

She walked the same path through the forest. She plucked the same flowers and herbs, admired the same scenes. Long ago, she had envied the famed automatons of Hephaestus, machines crafted perfectly in the imperfect image of mortals, content to carry out the same procedure forever. Her envy had dissipated as she herself had begun to resemble these mechanical creatures. There was nothing to distinguish the two.

Calypso stopped by the edge of the lake. She set down the basket of fruits and vegetables she had picked. She did not need them, immortals never did, but they were a part of her routine, and so never to be missed. She stared out at the water.

Animals skirted the perimeter as they always did. Frogs and birds and spawn of the woodlands as old as the goddesses did, too, as they had done since time immemorial. They never touched the water. Calypso's reflection and the reflection of her home were clean and undisturbed – they had been for centuries. The wind that softly tugged her straw-coloured hair behind her ear seemed to have its purpose and left the water unmoving. Nature was itself an odd creature on this island.

The last person to have injected imperfection into the mirror image of the water had been her. Now, Calypso could scarcely remember what it felt like. She was surprised she even cared.

Surprise, she thought, *it's been a while.*

The notion amused her slightly. She picked up her basket and set off back to her cave. In the orange light of the sun, she walked her path, beaten down by time.

* * *

Calypso woke once more. The sun had not yet risen, and there was but a sliver of moonlight glimmering in from the world. Still, she stared at the crystals above her, as bright and purposefully beautiful as ever, bathing in their own special light.

She thought again of the water, of her reaction. Emotions, faint, yet such as she had not felt since the man. The image of him in her mind dissipated before it could fully materialise, a defence mechanism manifested in his wake. She rose from her bed.

Calypso dressed herself and once again picked up the basket before stepping from her cave into the early morning air. After a lifetime of constants, there was an intangible difference about today. Nothing she could see or sense at all, it was a feeling. She was feeling again. Calypso smiled a hollow smile.

Walking the path she knew so well into the forest, she once again did as she always did. But again, something was different. She waded through the underbrush, into an expanse of tree canopies and birdsong, marvelling at her home's beauty in a way she had not done for most of her immortal memory.

A paradise was what one made of it. Perfection does not necessitate it; it is the person who must. Ogygia had not been her paradise in a long time.

As she reached the lake once more, she thought of today and yesterday and the day before and all those that seemed one and the same. She thought about the last time paradise had meant something to her. In an instant all the memories came flooding back. Odysseus. Their time together had been bliss. Gods always chase the next amazing thing, their next high, but he was hers. And he was enough.

When he was taken away – when he chose to go, she reminded herself – that was the last time she had harboured any emotion at all. Despair at losing her love. Vitriol for the hypocritical gods. Happiness to bitterness to nothing. But now, something.

Odysseus was gone now. Dead, most likely. Calypso remained.

She was as constant as time, as her imprisonment. She looked again at the island around her, reflected in the still lake. She was as constant as perfection. Recognising that beauty, that perfection in herself and her home, a sense of empowerment surged through the goddess.

Ideas of her own irrelevance that had pervaded her mind for millennia were washed away. In their place, Calypso thought of Ogygia. She was alone. She was home. Both were true, and neither detracted from her significance. Calypso was exactly as important as she needed to be. This island served as a reminder of that fact.

She knelt and touched a finger to the water. She watched her features gently warp as ripples extended outward and faded, something impermanent yet undeniable – her doing.

Calypso was in a prison, yes. She had supported the wrong side in a war she scarcely understood, and had been sentenced to her island, in solitude.

As she walked back through the forest, the goddess stopped and looked down. Countless footsteps echoed the lifetime of journeys she had made in this one place. She followed them back to her cave, the crashing of the waves behind her as she entered, calming her racing mind.

Calypso woke up, once again in no hurry to start her day. She lay peacefully in bed, watching the ceiling, finding comfort in the patterns of light that danced above her on the crystals. She rose. The day was the same, but she was different. As much as that first part was true, so too is her difference. Not growth, perhaps, but *change*.

In the arch of rock that held at bay the outside world, Calypso stood. She stared out across the sea and the sky, searching for nothing. She was content. Against the will of primordial forces and intentions, she was happy.

Calypso considered the field of blue once more before walking out and stopping in front of the forest – her paradise. She smiled. A real smile, so powerful in its simplicity. Then Calypso stepped forward and did as she always did, save for the smile. That was new, and here to stay.

* * *

Writing that story required a level of perspective on my part I hadn't thought would be necessary. The reason is as simple as it is benign – that which comprises Calypso's curse is something I'm drawn to: independence and, to a lesser degree, solitude. Save perhaps a dozen people at most, there are few I can stand being around. I am not a people person. I find it immensely hard to connect and establish relationships, and am in awe of my past self for doing that but leaving no trace of instructions.

So far, all I've been able to deduce as necessary is time spent in someone's company, which makes me cringe to such a degree I never consider it an option. Moreover, another staple of Calypso's imprisonment is the routine, the endless cycle that drives her life on Ogygia. I love routine. I crave it – any consistency in my life I can muster – but am only afforded a few weeks at a time at most. The point is, I had to try hard to relate to the character of Calypso, rather than her circumstances.

That being said, here's a short essay/story from my life that I had in my mind while writing about Calypso.

* * *

The sun was starting to dip in the sky. It was early afternoon, but that never counted for much in an English winter. I had just woken up and was in no mood to start my day. Nevertheless, I did. I had things to do, and I loved that. Necessity and deadlines fuel me – as much as I tend to resent them, they are far more valuable to me than I could ever give them credit for. A short half an hour later, I was ready to actually begin.

I had one lecture that day, but it wasn't for another hour or two. I could have prepared for it, sure, but there was no reason to. I had, by this point, become disillusioned with my academic career at university, and was beginning to question my place there entirely. Besides, the lecture was a philosophy one – I wasn't going to get called on, and even if I were, feigning deep thought or confusion was perfectly acceptable, and practically second nature.

I'd woken up once today already. An Arabic lecture with an unfortunately far more participatory professor, who unfortunately had the good habit of engaging with his students. Thankfully, more eager classmates of mine were always there to occupy his attention. Rolling out of bed slowly, I logged into the class virtually. My professor sat in an empty classroom not two hundred metres from my door, as he always did, his students shuffling in online. What I hated about online learning was how much it enabled my complacency. What I loved about it was that mere attendance was the lowest bar and criminally easy to achieve. So, I clicked the requisite link and promptly fell back asleep.

Lunch was what it always was: a packet of pasta that took as much effort to cook as it did to eat. Still, it was reliably good and simple, and that was more than enough for me. I washed the four utensils required to prepare it and headed out the door.

I hurriedly rushed back in, though, fetching my coat. The pale sun had appeared deceptively warm in my window, but that goes to show my baseless optimism. Finally, out in the world, I started walking. Exploring London on foot had very quickly become my favourite thing to do. I'd plot a destination far away and follow the map there. One time was enough for me to learn the route, and before I knew it, I had several long walks stored in my brain and was always eager to don my well-worn headphones and set off.

Today was one of my shorter ones. As much as I didn't find the prospect of the philosophy lecture exciting, I knew

I had to attend – to appease the chronic completionism within me more than out of any sense of academic duty. As previously stated, I had none.

Walking is one of a handful of habits I have been able to translate into the different environments I find myself populating, and for that, I value it all the more deeply. Whenever I have found myself without consistency or mental comfort, returning to it puts me at ease and motivates me in whichever way I may need it.

Back in my neighbourhood, I sat in my philosophy lecture. I listened to my classmates articulate points none of us really understood. I took sparse notes that I knew I would never read again.

Being in the company of others was generally a rare occurrence at that time, and being in a situation with such low stakes, with my peers, was oddly comforting. That was the extent of my sociability, though. For the most part, it still is. Pleasantries and light conversations exchanged. Harmless. The manifestation of the high stakes I felt would come but a few hours later.

I was back in my room, catching up on TV. The sun had set hours ago, but it was still early. I hadn't looked at my class group chats in quite some time by that point, in fact I had muted most of them. The one that I hadn't, though, pinged for the first time in a month. A few people from my class were going to be at the social on campus.

My mind raced. Right in front of me was a social opportunity, something that I had begged for and then wasted so many times in my few months at university. The campus was a four-minute walk away. I decided I was going to go. I put on my hoodie and hurriedly preened myself. Before I had time to second-guess my choice, I was out the door. Not without making a quick stop, though.

I made my way to the kitchen and rummaged in my cupboard until I found it. A small bottle of vodka – the only alcohol I tolerated – that I had bought in my first week, certain it would come in handy once my role as the life of the party had been established. Twelve weeks later, it was still unopened. I stuffed it into the oversized pocket of my hoodie before stepping out the door.

From there, it was straight down the street and then I'd be there. I spent that short walk psyching myself up... or trying to. Picturing what it would be like and what I would do while at the same time trying not to think about it too much for fear of making myself anxious. Too late.

I walked into the building and asked a tired security guard where the social was. I was grateful he made no comment to my obtuseness as he pointed in the direction of the door, behind it a muffled sound of music. I walked in – again, completely unsure of what I was doing – and felt my heartbeat in my chest. Not pounding, just a general unsettling awareness on my part.

The room was split into two floors. The top one, where I now stood, was bathed in red light, which spilt in fragments down the stairs to the darker level I faced. I did a quick loop of the top floor, where not much was going on. Then, once again acting before I could overthink it, I walked downstairs. It was exactly what I thought it would be and wanted it to be. There was no pressure coming from anyone. Only from myself.

Just before my foot touched the last step, I panicked. *What was I doing here?* I thought. This wasn't safe for me. I sprinted back up the stairs with one, simple emotion inside me – fear. It devolved into overthinking and rationalisation as I left the building, turned the corner and headed home.

Not to sound too deterministic, but it wasn't my choice. The fear, my social shortcomings, any of what had happened that night. Once I was back in myself, I realised it was still quite early, and dejected though I was, I had so much time to kill.

I took out my phone and looked for movies that were playing in town. I was looking for something, anything to distract me and keep me occupied for a few hours, and catching a movie was always a good bet for me. I was in the heart of London, but I found an old favourite of mine playing an hour later, a couple of miles away.

A limited capacity for sociability can plague many people for many different reasons, but it comforted me to remember that the value I find in myself and what I can do is just as powerful.

Still shaken, but with the faintest hint of a smile on my face, I started walking.

Finis

Acknowledgements

My first extension of gratitude must go to the collaborative and creative voices of Jason Webster and Agustín Gonzalez, without whom I would have fallen at every single hurdle I faced, and whose patience and understanding are virtually unparalleled.

I would be remiss for not taking the time to mention Jerzy Juszkiewicz for making this book possible in many meaningful ways, and for providing a much needed outside perspective when I got too comfortable.

I am grateful to Sian for her eagle eyes and her proofreading skills that proved crucial – on several occasions – to making sure my first foray into the world of published writing didn't start with a dozen typos and deserved embarrassment.

And, of course, to Baba and Mummy, whose blind faith and optimism and cajoling I have eventually come to see as the boons they were. Your advice was always appreciated – perhaps not followed directly, but always served as learning opportunities. Please excuse my cold temperament, and know that your words mean more to me than you could ever know.

The Author

BORN INTO A celebrated family of writers and storytellers, Timur Shah has been fascinated with ancient mythologies since early childhood. He was raised at Dar Khalifa, a rambling mansion set squarely in the middle of a Moroccan shantytown, as well as in India, and at boarding school in England.

Through his love of folklore, and during travels through Europe, Africa and the Far East, Shah has learned to appreciate the world through a lens of his own – one shaped by an abiding love affair with myth and legend.

www.ingramcontent.com/pod-product-compliance
Lightning Source LLC
Chambersburg PA
CBHW051724040426
42447CB00008B/970